CW00926539

# GOBOWEN TO EVEREST
## A Himalayan Journal

———

**Dave Andrews**

Published by: David Andrews (Offa Books)
ISBN 978-0-9932975-1-9

Text and photographs: David Andrews
Email: dand103750@aol.com
Website: www.oswestryround.co.uk
Typesetting and layout: PSCD Paul Seager Creative Design
Printed by: WPG Ltd, Welshpool

Other books by Dave Andrews

In English
The Oswestry Round (with Jane Trudgill) - Offa Books, 2015
Welsh Mountain Walks - Lolfa Press, 2000
The Welsh One Hundred - Lolfa Press, 1999

In Welsh
Cant Cymru - Lolfa Press, 1998
Llais y Llosgwr - Lolfa Press,1994
Y Twll yn y Wal - Lolfa Press, 1992
Dewch i Chwarae: Karate a Jiwdo - Lolfa Press, 1987
Ymwelwyr Annisgwyl a storïau eraill - The Welsh Academy, 1980

# Foreword

This book is based on a diary I kept while I was on a trek in Nepal. Like so many people, I'd always wanted to see Everest with my own eyes. An opportunity arose out of the blue. I met Brian Blessed at Theatr Clwyd in Mold where he was giving a talk. He was about to embark on the second of his three attempts on Everest with an international team of climbers who were looking to recruit a small support team to travel as far as Everest Base Camp. He put me in touch with the expedition organisers. So a chance conversation led to a big adventure.

The diary lay on a shelf for a long time after I came home from Nepal, together with photographs and newspaper cuttings about the expedition. In late 2016 I decided to write it up in book form to raise money for two cancer charities, Cancer Research UK and Lingen Davies Cancer Fund. The first of these is a national charity and a household name - and rightly so - but the second is a local charity which is not as well known as it ought to be or as it deserves. Lingen Davies Cancer Fund has its office at the Royal Shrewsbury Hospital. Nearby is the Lingen Davies Centre, where cancer patients from Shropshire and Mid-Wales are treated.

I was treated in the Lingen Davies Centre for prostate cancer in 2014. As I wrote in a letter of appreciation to the hospital's Chief Executive following my initial treatment, I found all the staff at the Centre courteous, friendly, helpful, considerate and caring. Throughout the seven weeks and more of my treatment they were thoroughly professional in their approach and at the same time sensitive to my needs. They always addressed my concerns about treatment and answered all my questions. In short, I felt very well taken care of. But as I say to groups whenever I'm giving a talk about my books or about the work of the Centre, I sincerely hope you never need to step through its doors.

Writing books is one way I have of giving something back to the Lingen Davies Centre. There have been other ways too. My wife Jane and I have organised charity concerts, for example, and I've represented

Lingen Davies Cancer Fund in a number of running events including the Shrewsbury Half Marathon and the London Marathon. I've also represented LDCF at various functions. Some readers will know about my last book, The Oswestry Round, and about the Oswestry Round Challenge which is based on it. These have also raised money for LDCF and have, I hope, helped to raise its profile.

All the publication costs of this book have been covered with the assistance of friends. You can read about this in the 'Thanks' section which follows. As a result, all the money from sales - except any commission taken by booksellers - will go directly to Cancer Research UK and Lingen Davies Cancer Fund. Please encourage your friends to buy a copy! Copies can be bought at www.oswestryround.co.uk and all proceeds from on-line sales go to the two charities.

# Thanks

A book is never the work of just one person. Many people have helped me in the production of this one. I want to say thank you to everyone who has contributed.

First of all, I want to thank Angela Wagstaff. Angela was among the first to support the book financially, when it was little more than an idea. Always supportive and encouraging, she has discussed the project with me at every stage, usually in one of Oswestry's many cafes - which I've now come to know quite well - but also in my home. She kindly read the book in draft and suggested several valuable amendments. Thank you, Angela.

Jennifer Holderness, through her own hard work, raised a considerable sum to help meet the production costs. She also helped with publicity and did much to promote the project in its early stages, often supported by her husband Paul. Jennifer's enthusiasm has been an inspiration to me. Hers has been another positive voice throughout the process.

I want to thank Neil Ruby, a great friend and ally, who has overseen all financial matters relating to this book in the same meticulous way as he did and continues to do with my last book, The Oswestry Round, and also the annual walking event based on it, the Oswestry Round Challenge (ORC). Neil has helped my projects in countless other ways, too numerous to list.

Two musician friends, Keith Offord and John Neilson, gave the project a great boost financially when they offered to donate their fee for a concert I organised for them to the book fund. The ticket money taken that evening was also paid into the fund and those present in the audience can accept my thanks for unwittingly helping me!

I would like to thank Oswestry Borderland Rotary Club who contributed to the cost of publication, just as they did in the case of The

Oswestry Round. Their support for my projects has been enthusiastic and continuous.

My good friends Dave and Nêst Thompson were the very first to offer financial support for this book when I casually mentioned at dinner one evening that I had an idea for a follow-up book to The Oswestry Round. Thank you both.

I want to thank fellow writer Trixie Roberts for using her talents as compiler of quizzes to help raise funds for the book. Another fellow writer, Ron Turner, kindly donated money from the sales of the electronic version of one of his novels.

I would also like to thank the team at Oswestry Library for their support with this project and with the Oswestry Round Challenge. Our town is very fortunate to have a resource of this quality.

I want to thank fellow members of the Oswestry Writers Group who were the first to hear several passages from Gobowen to Everest in draft form. Their feedback and comments during our regular meetings were all useful and always constructive.

This book also received financial support from other friends, family members and people I met for the first time after giving a talk about my plans for writing it. In this context I want to thank Jennifer Ager, Mr A Kincman, Debbie Marais, Mr Parker, Peter Trudgill and Juliet Trudgill. I also want to thank the various organisations who invited me to give these talks, including Oswestry U3A, Phoenix Group of Selattyn, Oswestry Borderland Rotary Club and Oswestry Public Library.

I want to thank Paul Seager of Paul Seager Creative Design for his time and expertise and also Gary Williams and the staff at Welshpool Printing Group.

Lastly I want to thank my wife Jane and those friends who helped me during the difficult period I went through following the shock of being diagnosed with prostate cancer. Your kindness helped me through that period. My recent writing projects have helped too, not least because through them I have made many new friends.

# Gobowen To Everest

It's late September but early morning. Very early. On the platform in Gobowen station, which at this hour seems rather like a cemetery with lights, a bitter breeze has cooled my enthusiasm for the trip ahead and I'm tempted to phone a taxi to take me home. Home to my cosy study; home to familiar surroundings; home to my books and hobbies; home to Jane. Another gust gets me rubbing my ears and suddenly, from the vapour of my breath, out pops the genie of conscience. 'You selfish so-and-so! Leaving your wife behind while you go off and pursue some pointless dream. All that way and all that money and effort just to see a mountain. Aren't there enough mountains for you here in Britain?' I feel the house key in my pocket.

For me, the hardest part of any journey has always been closing the door and turning the key. My hand hesitates momentarily and there are uncomfortable thoughts. Whenever you set off on an adventure, you're always leaving something behind – your family, your friends, perhaps the whole of your past life – and when you return home you won't be exactly the same person you were before you set out. The journey will change you. You realise this and all the time you also realise that the choice is yours. No-one is making you go, after all. The choice can seem an absurd one, even to yourself.

But I stay on the hard bench despite any misgivings and think of all the preparations I've been through for this trip. Hours of form-filling; applications for visas; medical tests and jabs; drawing up lists of clothing, equipment and the various drugs and medical stuff I'll need for a journey of nearly a month in remote, mountainous country where there are no roads or electricity, no Boots the chemist to pop into for things and no hospital or surgery for miles. Not to mention the extra training I've done to get myself fit for a trek to Everest Base Camp and beyond. The sound of the name Everest does the trick and the breeze around my ears no longer feels quite as cold. I think my conscience has gone back to sleep too.

The train trundles slowly into the station, reflecting my own lethargy, and as I haul my rucksack on board and search for an empty seat - there are plenty of them at this time of day - I feel slightly drowsy in the stuffily warm carriage. I think of Jane fast asleep still in the cosy bed I had to tear myself out of, a little over an hour ago. I can feel her warmth and have the smell of her in my nostrils. The names Jane and Everest ping-pong in my mind but I try to settle the issue once and for all by sternly reminding myself that sometimes you have to be adventurous and that, besides, I'm very fortunate to be able to go to Nepal and see Everest with my own eyes. For all that, a suspicion crosses my mind that actually I may have fallen victim to authors who delight in writing enticing descriptions of far off lands and recording the heroic deeds of real adventurers. At this point, unable to cope with the idea that I'm neither a real adventurer nor a good husband, I let my rucksack drop heavily on the floor, curse the authors of every book I've ever read about Everest and search for the empty note book in which I will keep a diary of my trip.

As the train pulls out of the station, a new wave of excitement breaks over me. There's no going back now. The decision is made and the trip is underway. As the doubts subside, I realise once more that awaiting me are fantastic vistas and experiences I shall probably never forget. In my mind, I clearly see once again one of the hundreds of photographs I have seen over the years of Mount Everest extending upwards almost infinitely, the snow thick and deep on its ridges and faces, the sky cloudless and blue overhead. I see the fearful Khumbu Icefall, whose fickle and ever-changing, twisted surface makes it the most dangerous obstacle to climbers on their way to the summit from the Nepal side of the mountain.

But now a different kind of fear grips me, one that has been lurking in the back of my mind for months. What if Everest is under cloud by the time our little group reaches the Khumbu valley after almost a fortnight walking in? What if the monsoon season isn't quite over by then? The thought that I've spent so much time preparing for this journey, not to mention the money it is costing me, and that I might not even get to see Everest at all during our stay in the Khumbu area is almost unbearable. I know this thought is going to keep me awake throughout the approach trek. We will only have two nights in the famous valley and there will only be one proper opportunity to get a really good view of Everest itself, when we climb the mountain called Kala Pattar on the opposite side of the valley. From Base Camp, the summit of Everest is hidden by ridges and the icefall.

The other major matter that troubles me now and which I know will continue to trouble me throughout the approach to Everest is whether I will be able to adapt to the lack of oxygen as we climb higher. I've read enough about high altitude sickness and death through pulmonary oedema to make me very uneasy - uneasy enough not to have mentioned these things at all to Jane. I remember arriving in Colorado for the first time, many years ago, and finding it hard to breathe even in the foothills of the Rocky Mountains above the town of Boulder, at about 8,000 feet above sea level. It took me a week or so to acclimatize properly, by walking high during the day and descending at night-time to sleep. Only then could I hope to tackle the mountain summits over 14,000 feet for which Colorado is famous. Even then, when I descended from these summits a headache was a clear sign that the lack of oxygen had affected me. On our way to Everest, we will have to walk and sleep above 14,000 feet for well over a week with only a minimum amount of time and opportunity to acclimatize. No-one can know in advance whether or not they will be able to acclimatize properly. This is what's so frustrating and frightening. Fitness has nothing to do with it nor the fact that you've been able to acclimatize on previous occasions. Edmund Hillary - who reached the summit of Everest in 1953 - was not even able to reach Base Camp at the foot of the Khumbu Icefall when he returned to Nepal just a few years later.

With these unsettling thoughts weighing me down I sink a little further into my seat in the stuffy carriage. I look through the window as the familiar villages and landmarks pass by and think once more about Jane at home alone. Together we have walked mountains all over the world - in France, Italy, Switzerland, Austria, Spain, America and New Zealand as well as Scotland, Ireland, the Lake District and Wales. It seems strange now to place my hand on the empty seat next to me.

But the train and I move onwards and as Gobowen grows further away I start to look ahead instead of backwards. My doubts slowly dissolve as morning progresses and in some strange and inexplicable way, my fear that I may not actually get to see Everest after all fills me with determination to give myself the best chance of doing so by following all the advice we've been given about acclimatization, diet, hydration and rest, and so make sure I can actually reach the Khumbu Valley. I know this challenge will drive me on when the hard work begins.

It's evening and I'm in my little room in a nondescript hotel near Victoria Station. By now, the morning time uncertainty which almost paralyzed me in Gobowen station has long since disappeared, like breath into the air, and when I was chatting with Jane on the phone earlier - possibly for the last time in a month - I could hear in her voice a level of enthusiasm for my adventure which made me feel rather ashamed that I'd been so negative myself. I knew I needn't worry about her being on her own either. She's strong and determined - more so than me, it seems - and she will fill her hours and days with her work and her many friends.

Earlier, over a solitary dinner in the hotel restaurant, I decided to pass the time by trying to remember as many as I could of the statistics and facts about Everest which I'd read over the years - its height and position, the names of its ridges and features, and the various dates associated with their discovery. But these mere facts soon gave way to the heroic stories of the mountaineers themselves. These stories, so familiar to me now, all flooded back into my mind at the same time - the early expeditions of the 1920s and 1930s on the mountain's northern side in Tibet and especially, of course, the unexplained disappearance of George Mallory and Andrew Irvine in 1924, one of the greatest mysteries of the twentieth century; the unofficial trips by eccentric individuals, some of whom lost their lives; the post-war British expeditions of the 1950s and how a team from Switzerland came within a whisker of reaching the summit in 1952, guided by Tenzing Norgay, the Sherpa who eventually reached the summit the following year with Edmund Hillary on the famous first recorded ascent with the British expedition led by John Hunt.

The 1953 expedition was the ninth British expedition during the decades when Britain enjoyed a virtual monopoly on the mountain, a monopoly only ended by that Swiss expedition in 1952. As the Swiss had already been granted permission by the Nepalese authorities to return for a further expedition to Everest, and as they had climbed higher on their first attempt in 1952 than the British had managed during their eight prior expeditions, the pressure was well and truly on the British expedition of 1953 to succeed at last. It had become, in the eyes of many, a matter of national and imperial pride at a moment when repeated failure meant that, in the words of Captain G. I. Finch - who had himself climbed to well over 8000 metres on the second British expedition in 1922 - "…we are beginning to make ourselves look very ridiculous".

As usual I linger over the story of the Deputy Leader of that successful British expedition in 1953, the Welshman Sir Charles Evans, later Principal of the University College of North Wales Bangor as it was called when I was a student there. Charles Evans and his climbing partner, an Englishman by the name of Tom Bourdillon, came very close to reaching the summit of Everest on 26 May, three days before Hillary and Tenzing. They were less than three hundred feet below the summit, they had made excellent progress, the weather was fine and almost everything was in their favour. Yet, for some reason, they turned around and came down, blaming their oxygen equipment. The official accounts skirt around this topic - as indeed they skirt around many awkward topics to do with personalities and decision-making - and so much of what actually went on remains unknown to the public. The focus in these official accounts was on the success of the expedition and on what can be achieved by determination, courage and team work. But Evans' decision remains a mystery to me and one that needs looking into further. Perhaps I'll delve into it deeper one day and write a book about it! Whatever the case, Evans and Bourdillon made a decision which condemned them to virtual oblivion whereas everyone today knows the names Hillary and Tenzing.

I remind myself how excited I would feel when I read accounts of the early adventures to the mysterious and forbidden lands of Nepal and Tibet, whose borders Everest straddles. In particular, I remember the daring - not to say outrageous - adventures of the extraordinary Captain John Noel who, in 1913, disguised as a native of India and accompanied by three native porters, journeyed illicitly into Tibet. His party avoided villages and settlements, carried their own food and kept to desolate areas where they saw only the occasional shepherd. He was the first Westerner to get within forty miles of Everest. Eventually he discovered his map to be hopelessly wrong and, with another range of mountains ahead of him and his resources dwindling, he could go no further. He later joined the official British expeditions of the 1920s as photographer and filmmaker. He was the last man to see Mallory and Irvine alive.

Before retiring for the night I decide to go through my baggage yet again, even though I must have checked it a hundred times before leaving home. I packed and re-packed everything myself and so it comes as no surprise to find that all is in order. I don't seem to have forgotten anything. I pull out my toilet bag and head for the bathroom. Inside the bag I find a short letter from Jane. In it she exhorts me to make the most of every moment of my adventure and reassures me that she will be fine. I'm moved by her choice of words but rather than dwell on the feeling I allow myself to smile at the fact that she somehow managed to slip her letter in there without my noticing.

# Saturday 25 September

There's nothing new to me about Victoria Station - nor about travelling through London for that matter - but as a merely occasional visitor I find the experience of being here exhilarating. All that coming and going. The toing and froing, the energy and the constant movement. The station reminds me of an ant colony as the people rush by and weave their way between each other, every one with their own agenda. They seem not to notice one another and yet, almost magically, seldom collide. It's tempting to see them as a moving, amorphous mass but if you have time to step back and observe - as I have this morning while I'm waiting on this bench for my train, munching my way through a bag of salted peanuts - and if you look closely at any particular individual you remember that each of these people has his or her own preoccupations, feelings and problems. How easy it would be though, in a situation like this, to forget that they all have a name and an individual identity. The pace of life is rather different in our little hamlet back home in Shropshire. I'm tempted to conclude that our quality of life is better too. But who's to say?

I wonder whether the bright atmosphere of this familiar station and all this frantic movement of people have done something to raise my spirits, shift my mood or set a different background tone for the day ahead. It's so unlike the tiny station of Gobowen where I was sitting yesterday morning with my gloomy forebodings. Well, whether or not it's the influence of the big city, I'm certainly in a good mood this morning.

As I stroll across the forecourt towards the trains, the pigeons scatter before me. The train has actually arrived already. This is a promising start and, as if to make my mood even better, the sun is now shining. I hold out my ticket for the ticket man at the gate. He takes it without looking at me or uttering a word. 'Miserable so-and-so,' I think to myself as I'm reminded of the cold, anonymous aspects of city life. Suddenly though - just as if he'd read my mind and wanted to upbraid me for my attitude - he raises his head and looks straight into my eyes. We linger briefly looking at each other. Then, with an exceptionally friendly smile, he says 'Good morning, sir. Have a nice day.' Mmm. Perhaps I'm the one who's a miserable so-and-so.

Something about the ticket man's hands reminded me of Jane's father's hands. This brought Jane to mind once more and as I walked along the platform I found myself searching instinctively in my pocket to make sure that her letter was still there. A silly thing to do in a way. A letter can't jump out of a zipped pocket after all.

Later, when I reached Gatwick, I went straight to the lounge where some of the other members of our group - there will be about fifteen of us altogether - had already started to assemble. I hate being late and despite the problems I had this morning getting a taxi from the hotel I'm pleased to find that I'm here in good time. Only a handful of my companions for the adventure ahead have arrived before me.

While we wait for the rest of the party to appear, we introduce ourselves briefly and start to get to know each other. Perhaps the anticipation and the excitement - and perhaps a certain amount of apprehension and the knowledge that we'll be travelling together for several weeks - makes us keen to break the ice and establish good relations. The first to introduce himself to me is Richard, a large, muscular fellow from Buckinghamshire, high-spirited and talkative, who seems to me full of self-confidence. In contrast I then meet Mark, a quietly-spoken, amiable soul from Leicestershire who chooses his words carefully. Next I meet John and Gwen who live in London and are both commercial bankers. They have a self-assured and rather prosperous air about them. I meet Phil and Elaine. Phil is very pleasant and shakes hands warmly with everyone but I notice Elaine raises only the faintest of smiles, just enough to be courteous. I also notice that she seems unabashed about complaining to Phil about this and that, even in front of us strangers. He smiles weakly at her but says nothing in response.

Then I meet Peter from Norfolk who I'll be sharing a tent with when we reach the Himalaya. I'm glad to say that I take to him immediately. He's quiet, intelligent and modest. He's well-spoken too and has a range of interests similar to my own. In no time at all we're comparing notes on popular and classical music, and he seems to like the same films as me as well. We also have a similar sense of humour and soon find ourselves laughing out loud about some silly scene in a film we've both seen. In fact, some of the others mistakenly assume we're old friends. I think Peter and I will get on well together.

The others arrive in dribs and drabs. Mainly in couples. There's Pauline and Terry from Yorkshire, down to earth, open and friendly. I think they're both teachers. There's another Yorkshireman too, Albert, a car salesman, who like me is travelling on his own. He, Pauline and Terry soon discover each other and start talking about the virtues of their beloved county of origin. Good for them, too. There are now about a dozen of us. We're still missing three according to our tour guide, Wendy, who will fly with us as far as Kathmandu. There, we will be meeting Vivienne, a well-known walking guide from Northumberland, who will lead us to Base Camp and beyond. That said, once we reach the village of Lukla, high in the Himalaya, we will also have the company of Lakpa, a renowned Sherpa mountain guide who has already been to the summit of Everest twice. It's very reassuring to know we're going to be in such experienced hands.

I still get an immense thrill from flying even though I've been on so many flights over the years. I find it hard to understand people who complain about how long it takes to fly to their destinations. How quickly we forget how fortunate we are! Not that long ago, this kind of journey would have been impossible for the vast majority of us. Had it not been for World War Two, I doubt whether my father, who was from a poor family in Devon, would ever have travelled in an aeroplane. My mother never went abroad throughout her life. But many people nowadays feel the same about a trip in an aeroplane as they do about a trip on a bus or a train. Yet the thrill of knowing that I - a mere land creature - can be amongst the clouds and travelling at over five hundred miles an hour still gives me a feeling of elation. How can anyone not appreciate and enjoy this?

Peter was sitting beside me on the plane. When we eventually got around to talking about what we did for a living he told me that he was a dustman. He probably spotted my hesitation before I told him that he was the first ever dustman I had met who spoke with a public school accent. He muttered something unconvincing in corroboration but I couldn't stop myself from laughing incredulously. He seemed rather sheepish for a while and sensing my scepticism eventually confessed, in lowered tones, that he was actually a doctor. He swore me to silence.

I agreed to keep his secret if he so wished but asked him why on earth he had tried to convince me that he was a dustman. His reply to this question perplexed me even more. He said that if he had told the truth and written on the application form for the expedition that he was a doctor, he would have been able to come on the trip at half price. I must have looked at him in astonishment and he added that he wanted to get away from his work while he was on this trip. He didn't want people running to him with their petty ailments, he said. 'But what if someone fell ill?' I asked, sensing that Peter was far too conscientious and caring a man to ignore anyone in distress. 'Surely your training and your medical instincts would kick in straight away?' 'Mmm,' he muttered, full of self-doubt. He fell silent for a few moments. Then he turned to me and said 'You haven't got any paracetamol have you? I've got a terrible headache all of a sudden.'

# Sunday 26 September

I don't enjoy travelling overnight. In fact, I detest it. I only got about four hours sleep on the aeroplane and that was following our one-hour stop in Dubai at one o' clock in the morning. And yet I was surprised to find that I awoke full of life and energy this morning, just as I did yesterday morning. It was probably due to the excitement of reaching a strange country, a country where I knew the customs and beliefs to be very different to our own.

Sure enough, something quite unexpected - something I'd certainly never witnessed before - happened on the way from Kathmandu airport to our hotel. We were in our tour bus, still on the outskirts of the city. As we approached a busy junction, two or three cows started to amble across the road in front of us. Perhaps they'd escaped from a nearby field, I thought. But there were no fences or hedges to be seen anywhere. It dawned on me as I watched the cows meander here and there along the road at a leisurely pace - quite untroubled by the traffic - that these animals were allowed to wonder as they wished. Indeed, one of the creatures decided to lie in the middle of the road about fifty yards ahead of us. The driver slowed down and surprised us all by coming to a complete halt in front of the cow. He surprised us even further by turning off his engine. We all stared at the scene and at each other. I had been used to seeing the odd sheep wander across the road back home but I'd never seen anything quite like this. The driver didn't sound his horn and was clearly happy to wait. In fact, we remained there for almost a quarter of an hour until madam decided that she wanted a better place to lie down than the main road into the city centre.

Eventually we arrived at our hotel which is on top of a hill on the outskirts of Kathmandu. As we made our way from the bus and walked through the garden and along the terrace we could see the city extending far away below us in all directions, filling the wide valley in which it stands. The Kathmandu valley is surrounded by low hills but today it lies in mist and we only get occasional glimpses of them. The monsoon season isn't quite over. It seems the weather patterns in this part of the world are fairly settled and predictable. When the rainy season ends, we ought to be able to rely on a period of cold but clear mornings in the mountains with cloud starting to build up towards the end of the afternoon. And it should be dry. I can only hope that the weather follows the expected pattern.

I may have awoken full of energy this morning but now the lack of sleep started to catch up with me. I was finding it hard to keep my eyes open as I sat in one of the deep, luxurious armchairs in the over-warm hotel lounge listening to our guide, Vivienne, who was explaining the arrangements for the next step in our adventure. I knew I should be giving her words my full attention, even though she was largely repeating things I had already read in the package sent out by our tour company. I did my best at least to give the appearance of listening carefully as she was issuing a variety of important instructions coupled with pointers on local etiquette, as well as warnings about some of the dangers we might face both here in this third world city and also later in the remote mountains. But I was struggling.

As my eyes grew heavier, I had to resort to pinching my thigh as hard as I could or poking myself in the ribs. At one point, when Vivienne mentioned my name in connection with Peter, I rose from my chair and went to sit next to him in a desperate effort to stay awake and to show Vivienne and the rest of the group that I was in fact taking in all the information. Moving about seemed to do the trick.

Vivienne emphasised that we should on no account drink any water which had not been boiled nor even put it in our mouths. The information pack we had received in advance had explained that water here carries all sorts of bacteria and diseases and I'd heard about several visitors to Nepal - which is one of the poorest countries in the world - who had forgotten or ignored warnings about the water and had spent the rest of their visit in hospital very ill. Indeed, it's not everyone who returns home alive after drinking the water and spending time in a Nepali hospital, where the medical care and standards of hygiene are far below what we're used to in our much-criticised NHS hospitals.

Vivienne suggested that those of us who had travelled on our own should share a bedroom in the hotel with our partners so that we could get to know each other a little before sharing the narrow confines of a tent together. Several members of the hotel staff now stepped forward to usher us to our rooms. As we rose to leave the lounge Vivienne said there was plenty of time to unpack, have a shower (for the last time until we return to the hotel in about three to four weeks' time) or catch up on some sleep. She emphasised once more that even in the shower we should be careful not to let the smallest amount of water enter our mouths. It would be really easy to forget this injunction when you're brushing your teeth, I thought. In our bedroom, I found myself repeating the words 'No water! No water!' whenever I went near the washbasin, hoping my brain would soon absorb the message.

Shortly before midday Peter and I made our way downstairs to join the others who were gathering in the hotel lounge for our trip into the city centre. Vivienne had arranged for a mini bus to take us down. I have to say that I've never seen such friendly and obliging people as the hotel staff - and none so obviously happy either. They give the impression that it's almost an honour to be able to serve us. They simply can't do enough for us. The driver of the mini bus had exactly the same attitude. And wherever we went in Kathmandu and its environs everyone seemed to have happy smiles. I felt slightly embarrassed about being so immensely rich compared to these people. Worse was the rather uncomfortable feeling that there was a legacy of empire in their perception of us and in their behaviour towards us - these wealthy, white Westerners.

In fact, more than one of our group has already muttered rather apologetically that they don't really like the idea that they will be paying someone else to carry their belongings for them once we get into the mountains. I think they feel it's exploitative or akin to slavery in some way. And to some extent I share their feelings. There's an inevitable master and servant aspect to our dealings with the people we have hired here to guide us and carry for us. We're two very distinct groups, different in colour, different culturally and certainly very different in terms of our relative wealth. Language separates us too and as no-one in our group has bothered to learn any Nepalese - beyond the universal greeting of 'Namaste' - we rely on those few locals who understand and speak a little English.

In essence, of course, ours is a commercial relationship in that we pay them for the services they provide for us. In some ways those services may appear demeaning to our modern Western sensitivities but the plain fact of the matter is that the inhabitants of this populous and poor country are very glad of the work we provide for them. Tourism is big business and it's the high mountains which attract most visitors to Nepal. The Himalaya is now a very popular destination for trekkers and climbers alike, and during recent years a number of agencies in the West have established adventure holidays in countries like Nepal. Unlike the countries of Europe, mountaineers have to pay to obtain a permit to climb some of the mountains of Nepal. In the case of the highest mountains, such as Everest, they pay a substantial amount. Climbers on the expedition associated with our trek to Base Camp will have had to pay a hefty five figure sum to be allowed an attempt on the summit of Everest and they won't be entitled to a reimbursement of any kind even if they fail to go beyond the Western Cwm, just above the Khumbu Icefall where Base Camp lies.

Inevitably, these journeys to remote mountain areas mean that you need to employ guides, porters, cooks and others from among the local population. I'll call them our support team. On an expedition like ours, there are more members of the support team than there are trekkers. These individuals may have to be away from home for much of the year but when working they can earn enough money to support their families during the months when there is little or no climbing and trekking.

In the meantime, our minibus arrives in the city centre and we step out into the maelstrom. Kathmandu is a real wonderland - for the outside observer at least. The place simply fills your senses. The smells, sounds and sights can overwhelm you. Narrow streets are jammed with a never-ending whirl of people and traffic, car horns being blown incessantly as the drivers weave their chaotic way through a flow of pedestrians and tricycle rickshaws, whose riders likewise ring their bells non-stop. There are statues, shrines, shops and stalls at every turn. The streets and squares are madly busy all the time. On the pavements lie baskets of fruit and vegetables, boxes of spices, piles of cloth and bags of rice all in colourful confusion. Everywhere you look you see people selling goods or offering services of all sorts - shoe cleaners, flute sellers with a hundred or more bamboo flutes sticking out on a pole in a way which reminds me of Jimi Hendrix's hair, and in one square I see a row of men, sitting with legs folded on a low wall, each with an old Singer sewing machine like the one my mother used to own when I was a boy. They offer to mend your shirts and your trousers for the equivalent of just a few pence in our money. Everything is so cheap here too. In one tiny and rather dingy looking street corner shop I bought a bottle of Coca Cola for the equivalent of about two pence.

As I walk around I see elaborately carved wooden balconies above tiny squalid shops, amazing temples and columns squeezed into small squares and overhead I spot a spaghetti-like tangle of wires and electricity cables dangling limply and looking not at all secure. And everywhere people, people, people. I've never seen so many people. Nor so many animals. Even in the middle of the city's busiest streets - not that I've seen any quiet streets here - cows and goats wander freely amongst the people and the cars as if this were the most natural thing in the world.

Most of the people here look poor, of course. And even though I've seen no signs of what you might call abject poverty in the centre of Kathmandu, we saw some ramshackle hovels on the city's edge which made you realise how fortunate we are back in the West to have solid, watertight houses. In the city centre, another thing which struck me was the extraordinary variety in the architecture. Next to a building which is typically Eastern in appearance you get a block of flats which is entirely Western. And then there are the highly ornate temples. Whatever may be the circumstances of the inhabitants - their poverty and their problems - these temples are a tribute to their inventiveness and their imagination, not to mention their supreme regard for religion. And the fact that Hindus and Buddhists share several of the gods and seem to live together quite harmoniously is a reminder that there are many things we in the so-called developed, civilized West could learn from these unassuming people.

I had read and heard a lot about Durbar Square and I was very keen to see it for myself. It didn't seem to be on our itinerary for the afternoon so I excused myself and left the rest of the group for a while. Armed with a map of the city which I'd picked up in the hotel, I set off on my own through the crowded streets in search of the famous square. You see, hear and smell so much more when you're on your own. Now, not needing to exchange small talk with people who were still new to me, I was able to let the city make its impressions on my senses.

With the help of my map I find Durbar Square with no difficulty. This is the heart of the old city where there's a wealth of temples and remarkable old buildings including the former royal family palace. It's a place where I would have loved to linger for hours. You get a strong flavour of the unknown East here, you feel the pulse of this ancient city as you wander at a leisurely pace between the striking temples and watch the monks in their colourful robes and the ordinary people of the city going about their daily lives. Not far away is Freak Street which got its name when Kathmandu became the destination for hippies during the 1960s.

The rest of the group found me as I was trying to take a photo of one of the temples in Durbar Square. I'd been there for about twenty minutes trying to take this particular photograph. It isn't that I'm a perfectionist or a meticulous photographer. It was merely that each time I picked up the camera, an old gentleman in rags would deliberately stand in front of me. He would place himself about six feet away from me, stand upright with a look of pride on his face and stare straight into the camera. He seemed to know precisely where to stand to have his picture taken. I was confused and more than a little embarrassed as I couldn't work out what his motive was. He had no begging bowl in his hand. Nor did he utter a single word. Every time I lowered the camera he would stand to one side and every time I raised it again he would be back. I had heard that some Buddhists believe that to have their photograph taken means to lose part of their soul. This was why I didn't wish to take anyone's picture without first asking their permission. It was obvious, though, that this old gentleman wasn't at all worried about losing his soul. Eventually I pretended to give up trying to take the photo and walked away with my fellow travellers but when I spotted the old fellow crossing the square in another direction I quickly ran back and took it. I turned to look at the old gent for one last time before he disappeared into the crowd. I had a slight feeling of victory but also a slight feeling of guilt. Perhaps I had actually taken something away from him after all.

There is at least one other place which any visitor to Kathmandu must see. This is the gompa or temple at Swayambhunath. It is among the oldest religious sites in Nepal, dating perhaps from about the beginning of the 5th century. Although the site is considered Buddhist, it is also revered by Hindus. It stands a little way outside the city actually. It's just as well that we have a hotel mini bus at our disposal. The building itself is well worth seeing - especially the enormous eyes of the Buddha painted on all four sides of the tower of the gompa. The eyes seem to follow you everywhere. But unlike the God of the Christian world - or at least the idea of him presented to me when I was a child - he isn't watching to make sure you don't misbehave but in order to look after and protect you. That's how one of the temple guides explained it to us anyway.

But the thing which is truly memorable about Swayambhunath is the many monkeys which wander all over the site - and completely freely of course. In fact the temple is often called the Monkey Temple. By now we have started to realise that animals are treated here in Nepal not only with respect - not just as fellow creatures with what we in the West would probably call rights - but also with reverence as many of them are associated with religion and with specific gods. There are numerous sculptures of animals to be seen on temples all over the city which represent the gods of the various religions.

To come back to the monkeys at Swayambhunath - well, they're mischievous to say the least. Troublesome is probably a better word. We had been warned not to wear or carry anything which could easily be taken by them - neither a hat nor a scarf - and that we should keep a firm grip on our cameras and our bags. It's no laughing matter after all to see your precious belongings being carried off for the sheer fun of it and being left dangling around a pole or a cable fifty feet up in the air or being flung from a high wall onto a spot where you have no chance of reaching them before they're picked up by another monkey. So it pays to be wary. As long as you protect your things you will find the monkeys amusing and entertaining rather than maddening. They remind me of Gremlins or a group of primary school children let loose in a toy shop.

I was still thinking about the playful monkeys at Swayambhunath and all the wonders I'd seen during my first day in Nepal as I was brushing my teeth in our hotel bedroom this evening - using bottled water of course. At this point, as we were winding down and getting ready for a night's rest, Peter started quizzing me about my home and family. It suddenly occurred to me that it was still less than two days since I'd been sitting in Gobowen station feeling anything but adventurous, to my shame, and yet I've already seen enough to justify a trip to a far off country. Travel seems to confuse your sense of time somehow and the effect for me was heightened by being in a so-called Third World country, where there are so many challenges to my fundamental assumptions and to my view of the world.

As I was thinking about an answer to Peter's last question about my family, I bent my head instinctively towards the tap to have a final rinse. Luckily I remembered Vivienne's injunction just in time and pulled away sharply, as if I'd seen a snake or as if the water itself were poison. Which it is, in a sense. 'No water! No water!' I yelped and reached for another of the bottles of water which the hotel staff had left in our room. Even then I checked that the seal hadn't been broken as Vivienne had warned us to do. My hand was visibly shaking as I realised that I'd come very close to potentially ruining the expedition for myself even before it has got properly underway.

Looking back at all the wonders I've seen today, I couldn't help feeling that I'd like to spend another day or two wandering at a leisurely pace through the amazing and colourful streets of the capital and take my time to explore the other towns in the Kathmandu valley - Patan and Bhaktapur. At the same time, I'm impatient to reach the mountains I've travelled here to see. As I pull the sheet and blanket over me, and say goodnight to Peter, I can only hope the weather will be in our favour tomorrow and that we'll be able to fly to Lukla, where our adventure begins in earnest.

# Monday 27 September

It was a very early start. The alarm went off at 4.30 and Peter and I were soon walking busily about our little room and trying not to get in each other's way. By shortly after five o' clock we were downstairs having breakfast with the rest of our group. The conversation was muted. Vivienne had warned us to be ready to leave the hotel by a quarter to six. It's important to leave in plenty of time, she says. Perhaps she's worried that there will be more cows on the road.

Our destination is the tiny mountain village of Lukla which stands at 11,000 feet, high in the foothills of the Himalaya. By flying there, we avoid having to do a week's trek from Kathmandu. On the down side, the additional days spent trekking would have given us all a far better chance of acclimatizing than we will now have by flying straight in to such a height above sea level where the air is so much thinner.

Soon we are heading off to the airport once again. It's difficult to believe we only arrived in Nepal yesterday. We've seen and experienced so many novel things already. I cast my eye around the group as we trudge towards the coach which is waiting for us outside, dragging our belongings. Most are half asleep or in a morning daze, moving silently, mechanically. Only Richard appears to be talking and even he's speaking in unusually low tones. I'm not sure anyone is listening to him. Certainly no-one is responding. But his irrepressible need to communicate may be very useful later on in our adventure.

It's a beautiful morning which lifts our spirits and boosts our hopes of getting away. Someone says they've seen a forecast and that it promises to be a fine day. So although I feel there's a great deal more to see here in the capital, I'm also relieved to know we have an excellent chance of heading up to the mountains. In fact I can't wait to get there. It would be very frustrating to have to remain here and lose a day from our trek. To do that would put a lot of pressure on our itinerary, with less time to get used to the lack of oxygen at altitude. The sooner we can start the process of acclimatizing the better.

The reason the weather is so critical now is that the aeroplane we will be taking has no radar equipment on board. The pilot will be relying on sight alone. That's how primitive and risky the situation is. If the pilot can't see the mountains and pick out certain landmarks or if the weather were to change suddenly and visibility becomes poor, we could quickly find ourselves in a precarious situation. I try not to think about it.

Once at the airport there was time to quickly write a half dozen or so postcards and post them before the plane arrives to carry us off to a place where, for us, there would be no communication with the outside world for several weeks. Peter takes a seat automatically at my side - as if we're already inseparable - and he too starts scribbling a number of cards. There's a concerned look in his eyes this morning for some reason. He seems preoccupied. He's very quiet too. I ask him whether he slept well. He answers briefly that he did.

After what seems like a long wait, suddenly we're told that our aeroplane is ready for us. Everyone gets up immediately, puts away their odds and ends and picks up their luggage. With the others I make my way from the departure lounge, aware that I'm feeling a little apprehensive. Perhaps I'm worried that I'm choosing of my own free will to travel to a place I may never be able to return from. And I'm actually paying to get there! Then, when I spot the tiny aeroplane which was waiting for us, looking completely out of place amid all the normal passenger jets, I suddenly remember the caring eyes of the benevolent Buddha on the gompa in Swayambhunath. I feel sure I've seen lorries bigger than the aeroplane now standing before me on the runway. It appears comical among these other aircraft and gives the impression of being a model aeroplane or a toy. It looks flimsy too and it's difficult to believe that it could actually take off and, even if it did, that it would be quite safe in the air.

Of course, these are just groundless impressions, I tell myself, but going up the short flight of small steps into the narrow fuselage - which seemed more like the inside of our mini bus - added to the uneasiness produced by these initial impressions. The roof was low and it wasn't possible to stand up straight. The seats were narrow and we were crammed very close together. Because the plane was so cramped and small, you somehow felt much more aware of the outside world than you would in a standard aeroplane, rather like being in a tent compared to being in a house. You couldn't ignore the sound of the engine either - yes, just a single engine - as it was so loud that we had difficulty hearing each other speak. The vibrations made the whole aeroplane shake, adding to the general nervousness that people attempted to conceal by giggling and by making jokes and facetious remarks in a natural attempt to deflect their genuine disquiet.

The plane seemed to have no cabin door and we could see the pilot in the cockpit. Straight away I noted that there was just one pilot, with no second officer. I heard Richard muttering some flippant - and rather silly - remark to some of the other males on board when he noticed that the pilot was a woman. Obviously this was entirely unjustified but it seemed to help some of the tougher types to deal with being on this bone-shaker and facing up to the fact - as you always must when boarding any aeroplane - that you're now entrusting someone else with your very life. The feeling of vulnerability is reduced on a larger aircraft but now I was having to face up to the fact that I would soon be airborne in what seemed to me little more than a garden shed with wings. A noisy and shaky garden shed at that.

It's strange how people deal with nerves and the feeling of being in danger. No-one was willing to come out with it and say they were scared but the unease among the group was palpable. I persuaded myself that the pilot was bound to know what she was doing and reminded myself that she had probably done this trip many times before. So I sat back quietly in my seat to enjoy the ride. Peter sat next to me still looking preoccupied. The noise from the engine - already loud - became a lot louder as the pilot revved it up and the plane started to trundle slowly along the runway. As our speed increased so did the nervous laughter and chattering on board. For some reason our situation brought to mind one of those scary rides at Alton Towers on the only occasion I'd ever been there, which was with a group of children from the school where I was teaching at the time. I couldn't recall the name of the ride but I remembered that we soon found ourselves advancing slowly in the dark before coming to a halt. It was pitch black and I couldn't see anything, not even the people sitting around me in the carriage. It really was quite scary. Then came a sudden vertical drop and a great deal of screaming. For my own good, I think, I now decided to dismiss this particular recollection from my mind. In the meantime, our plane was picking up speed as it rattled along the runway and the on-board laughter reached a squeaky crescendo - of relief I believe - when it eventually left the ground. My stomach churned a little and soon my ears popped. We were on our way.

Once you're in the air, there seems to me little point in worrying about whether or not you're going to reach your destination or whether the engine is going to fail. So I looked down on the urban sprawl of Kathmandu as we gained height and the plane glided outwards towards the green and fertile foothills surrounding the city. Because there was no cabin door we were also able to see the view ahead of us, just as if we were travelling in a car or bus. It wasn't long before we got our first clear, distant view of the high chain of snow-covered mountains we were aiming for. They seemed formidable - intimidating even - but at the same time enticing. Exciting. Beckoning. At last we were heading straight for the Himalaya.

Needless to say, the pilot knew exactly what she was doing. I found her calm approach reassuring. But what a difficult job she had. Somehow she was able to pick out individual mountains and other visual clues which she relied on to enable her to navigate her way towards Lukla, a tiny village quite impossible to spot in this enormous landscape. As we settle down to the flight the chatter becomes quieter, though at the same time I can still hear the excitement and the anticipation in people's voices. Only Elaine, I notice, seems lacking in enthusiasm for our journey and for the stupendous scenery. I catch her words now and again as she continues to complain to Phil about something or other. Phil has his arms folded and looks straight ahead at the snow-covered giant mountains of the Himalaya. He looks relaxed.

Like me, Peter is absorbing the scenery. He offers an appreciative comment now and again, as do I. I feel comfortable in his company. We can speak or not speak, just as we choose. Richard is talking to the charming Mark who, I suspect, is hearing rather more than he would wish but he's such an affable, patient fellow and seems happy to let Richard talk at him. Gwen and John are chatting away quietly to each other. They seem very close. I try to imagine what this experience means to two city types who spend much of their time in front of computer screens trying to earn huge sums of money for their banks. They have little experience of hill walking, they tell me, but I know they've been on adventure holidays all over the world together. They always appear calm, relaxed and happy.

Although there's no co-pilot on the aeroplane, there is however a stewardess. This seems really surprising and I can't help wondering whether it isn't another example of needless pandering to Westerners. Wasn't she merely taking up space on a crowded plane, I wondered. She had welcomed us on board when we climbed the steps but in my nervousness I'd then forgotten about her. About half way through the flight she suddenly reappeared from the back of the plane in her very smart uniform and beautifully turned out, holding a small tray of fruit-flavoured hard-boiled sweets wrapped in cellophane. I chose a red one. Once she had been around us all, she retreated to the back of the plane and sat on her own. I couldn't help thinking that they could have left a tray of sweets for us somewhere on the plane and spared her the need to fly back and to between Kathmandu and Lukla. There again, I reminded myself, this did at least provide her with employment.

We watched through the cockpit window over the next half hour or so as the high snow-covered mountains, which had seemed so far away when we first got on board, gradually grew nearer and nearer. They were still some way off though when the landing strip at Lukla finally came into view some way ahead and far below us. Straight away I sensed the tension increasing once again among us Westerners. There seemed to be good grounds for our misgivings. For one thing the landing strip was nothing but a short, muddy scratch on extensive green-brown slopes. It seemed an impossibly small target to land a plane on. At the lower end of the runway we could see a deep, dark, precipitous gorge which the pilot would have to get her aircraft across on her approach. It was an intimidating sight and people started murmuring apprehensively. I don't know whether he was aware of it but Peter was leaning against me slightly, as if for reassurance.

As we started the very long descent I found myself looking at the pilot and drawing on her calmness. It had by now become very quiet on board. Even Richard was silent. We all sat stock still in our seats, hardly able to believe that a safe landing could possibly be accomplished. I suspect too that we were all afraid of doing anything at all that might distract the pilot at this crucial point. The closer we got to the runway the more impressive became the jaws of the gorge below. There was a vertical cliff of at least a thousand feet ahead of us and it was clear at once to all of us that one mistake here would mean certain death. We could now also see that the runway was no more than a field - with no tarmac or man-made surface of any kind - and that it wasn't flat either. In fact it was on a slope which ran steeply uphill from the precipice towards the village. This was going to be no ordinary landing. It didn't help either that as we got closer we could actually see the remains of other aircraft scattered here and there along the edge of the runway.

I was thinking of Alton Towers again as we descended gradually towards the vertical drop into the dark - almost black - gorge. It was just possible to see how frighteningly deep it was and it came as a huge relief to feel, once we were about half way across, that whatever were to happen now - engine failure, the pilot suddenly passing out or whatever other terrible scenario my troubled brain was busy imagining - the sheer impetus of the plane was bound to carry us beyond the chasm and onto the far side. I had decided that a crash landing on the so-called runway would at least mean we were more likely to survive. I'm sure the pilot pulled back the throttle at this point but to me it didn't seem as if we were slowing down at all. The ground was approaching fast and the steep rise ahead in the runway made a crash landing seem inevitable. I had my eyes fixed keenly on the slope in front of me, struggling to believe that anyone could land a plane on such a steep gradient or that this could now end in anything except disaster.

In fact, our pilot made a perfect landing. There were spontaneous loud cheers of relief from everyone when we touched down. We all clapped enthusiastically too. The pilot probably thought we were just crazy Westerners. Perhaps she was used to this kind of applause. Who knows? All I can say is that her flying skills and that flight made an indelible impression on me. Soon we were standing on the grassy runway taking in deep breaths of delicious mountain air, glad to be alive. With our feet back safely on the ground once more, the dangers of the trek ahead of us - the glacier crossings, the gigantic ice towers on the Khumbu glacier known as seracs, liable to collapse without warning, and even the dreaded altitude sickness and the horror of pulmonary oedema - didn't seem quite so worrying.

---

So here we are in the village of Lukla, eleven thousand feet up in the Himalaya. As I look around at my new surroundings I feel as if I've stepped out of the Tardis and into a scene from centuries ago. It's disconcerting to say the least. If Kathmandu felt to me like a city far removed from the modern world, Lukla feels as if we've taken a further huge step backwards into conditions which remind me of the Middle Ages as described in school history books. I look back at the aeroplane which I had such misgivings about travelling on and watch as it turns around on the runway to head once more for Kathmandu. As I watch it, I find myself feeling abandoned.

I linger there as the plane accelerates down the runway and takes off. I want to wave at it but I don't. I keep watching until the tiny spot disappears from view over the high hills on the opposite side of the gorge. I feel intensely aware that I've been deposited in a totally unfamiliar, remote and alien place and that there's now no getting away. I turn to catch up with the rest of my group and find that Peter too - as well as a few of the others - has been watching the plane's departure wistfully. It seems for a moment to symbolise the modern, technological world we've elected to leave behind.

And now for the first time in my life I feel a profound sense of isolation - though not loneliness - which is disturbing and makes me feel insecure too. During my life I have often stood alone on mountain summits and in remote places which I know would have made many feel the kind of distress which sometimes comes with being far away from other people. The presence of others can provide a feeling of security. Being on my own has never bothered me though. In such remote places I was always aware that I was having to depend on my own resources and that there was no-one I could turn to for help if I needed it. But this was the first time I could remember feeling so completely dependent on the kindness and goodwill of strangers.

I take a few steps uphill from the landing strip and almost immediately I feel short of breath. I realise that my heart is beating faster too. At 11,000 feet up in the Himalaya our group all find the air thin and we struggle to walk the hundred metres or so to the tea house where we're to assemble. Standing outside the tea house - a large wooden building on the edge of the village - is the group of Sherpas who will be guiding us and taking care of us and also the porters, who are clearly of a different ethnic background to the Sherpas. The porters will be carrying most of our belongings as well as the goods and materials we will need for the journey towards Everest. The Sherpas and porters together outnumber us by at least two to one, it strikes me. The porters stand in a single large group, separate from the Sherpas, and watch us intently as we approach. They seem uneasy, perhaps suspicious. It doesn't feel like a friendly welcome. But we're entirely in their hands now and I hope we soon get a chance to establish cordial relations with them.

As we approach these strangers, I become aware of some instinctive reactions which I know I should resist. It has something to do with being foreign or perhaps with seeing foreigners, with being in a strange land, with being outnumbered, with feeling insecure and unsafe, with feeling that I might be physically vulnerable or threatened or called upon to defend myself. I feel ashamed of these reactions and try to put them to the back of my mind. I then realise I have my hand in my pocket and am clutching the key to my house.

Fortunately we don't have to wait long before being introduced to our support team. We all step inside the tea house together and in a large room we sit at solid wooden tables and wait for the formalities to begin. Our guide Vivienne introduces Lakpa, the head Sherpa. He smiles broadly and says a few words in his broken English. He strikes me straight away as a modest and friendly man and I decide immediately that I'd like to get to know him better. The atmosphere becomes a little more relaxed and even though we're not able to speak to the Sherpas or porters in their own language or languages, there's a palpable thawing in the air as we all start to mingle and people nod, smile and shake hands. I remind myself that our own little group are still strangers to each other more or less and that we're only just beginning to get to know one another. Now there's a new, bigger adjustment to make at the same time. Apart from the language difference between us and our support team there are also cultural and other barriers to overcome, unfamiliar customs to learn and different sensitivities to adjust to. I think they find some of our behaviour amusing, particularly our reaction to the rather over-sweet tea which they offer us and which we are too polite to refuse.

After half an hour or so, once the formalities and introductions are over, some of our group decide to go outside and explore the village and its surroundings. We wonder about with our cameras, all of us keen to start a photographic record of our trek. Lukla has the drab look of poverty. The streets are muddy and stony. Many of the buildings are, in truth, no better than huts or hovels. Here and there, though, there are signs of relative prosperity, especially in the tea houses, erected or improved with money made from travellers such as us.

Here in the mountains we're very far away from the ordinary comforts we take for granted in Britain. There is no electricity of course and no water on tap. The locals see aeroplanes regularly but many have never seen a car or even a bicycle for that matter. There are no roads here. A network of ancient tracks links the villages. Animals carry goods which are too heavy or awkward for the people themselves to carry. In general though it's the people who carry everything - on their heads or on their backs, usually in enormous, sturdy, homemade wicker baskets. They all seem very strong and tough. Even some of the children we see are carrying huge loads. Life in the West is very easy in comparison. There's no popping out to the shop here. People grow their own food on any scrap of land large enough and flat enough for cultivation.

The local people are Sherpas. They look poor - as indeed they are - and yet those I saw seemed content. Everyone looked at us and many greeted us and approached us to say hello. Some showed great interest in Peter's personal listening device and wanted to touch it. We knew we had no reason to fear for our belongings. Crimes such as theft are virtually unknown among these people even though the temptations, you would think, must be very strong. The camera around my neck - which is not an especially expensive one - is worth six months' salary for some of our Sherpas.

My camera drew a lot of attention, especially amongst the children who clearly knew what it was for. As I tried to take a photo of the buildings on one side of the main track through the village, a little girl came and stood right in front of me in the same way as that elderly man in Kathmandu had done. She gave me a friendly smile. Once again I couldn't see why on earth she would want to be in any photograph I took as there was no prospect of her even seeing it. But after I'd taken her photo she disappeared and I was able to take my photo of the buildings. A few seconds later though she was back with her little brother in tow and I had to take a picture of the two of them together. As I looked at them through the viewfinder it struck me that all the children I'd seen on my walk around the village wore colourful, well-made clothes. They all seemed happy too.

The Sherpas are a people who migrated to Nepal from Tibet originally, crossing the high snow-covered passes from the north. They are quite different in appearance to our porters who are from further south and India. There's a system of hierarchies operating here which we from the West are largely unable to see, although I read a good deal about it before travelling to Nepal. It's clear though that the Sherpas are of a higher social standing than the porters. Within the Sherpa group there are further divisions of status, some to do with mountain experience alone, some to do with relative wealth and power. And just as is the case back home, who you know and who your relatives are also seem to be important factors. Lakpa and his brother certainly seem to be held in high esteem.

Lakpa is a likeable fellow. Like many of the Sherpas he has an ever-ready smile. In that regard he reminds me of the most famous Sherpa of them all, Tenzing Norgay, who climbed to the summit of Everest with Edmund Hillary in 1953. I tell him this and he tells me that he's related to Tenzing Norgay so the similarity is no surprise. Yet in one significant way he's different to his famous relative - Lakpa has been to the summit of Everest twice! This trip of ours to Base Camp and a little beyond should be a walk in the park for him.

As Peter and I make our way back to the tea house for an early lunch before we set off on our first day's trek, we pass a small group of dzos which are being loaded by some of our porters. These creatures are a cross between the yak and domestic cattle. Yaks are better adapted to higher altitudes and we will be encountering them later on in our trip. The dzos and yaks are the real beasts of burden hereabouts. The local HGVs.

After a leisurely lunch we pick up our light day sacks and get ready for the first stage of our trek to Everest Base Camp. There's an air of excitement in the room as people do their final checks. Walking poles are extended, water bottles filled with water which has been boiled and allowed to cool. We're all set. It doesn't pay to hurry though. The effects of the thin air were noticeable even as we were strolling gently around the village before lunch.

People move outside and stand around in groups, waiting for directions from Vivienne or Lakpa. I notice that most of the dzos have already gone on ahead and that the last few are being loaded up before being sent on their way. Like the cows back home at milking time they seem to know which way to go and they leave the village unattended. Off they go and off go most of our worldly belongings on their backs.

Our trek on that first day was not a long one. The intention was to give us an opportunity to acclimatize. From Lukla the journey in the direction of Everest actually starts downhill, thankfully. Even so, because we haven't got used to the shortage of oxygen in the air it is still hard work. It's a strange sensation. You naturally expect to be short of breath from time to time when you go uphill but not when going downhill as we were now.

After a couple of hours of very gentle descent, we started to hear the distant roar of the water in the Dudh Khosi river. It certainly sounded full, even from afar. I had read that we would need to cross the river before reaching the flatter land where we were due to camp that evening, on the edge of a small hamlet. As our descent continued, the rumbling of the water grew ever louder and long before we could actually see the river I found myself wondering how wide it was going to be and what sort of bridge would be spanning it.

The bridge eventually came into view. It was a long one and nothing about its appearance or its position, just a few feet above the raging torrent, inspired confidence. The nervous talking and laughter started up, just as it had when we'd boarded our little aeroplane this morning. People seemed to slow down even further, as if reluctant to face what was inevitable. The bridge looked flimsy and makeshift to say the least. It was made of ropes and planks and it swung back and forth in the stiff breeze generated by the water below. The river is wide at this point and the water - which is very cold because it comes from a glacier higher up - flows fearfully fast. It was obvious at once that no-one who fell in could possibly be saved.

We soon realised too that some of the planks were missing, leaving a clear view of the mesmerizingly fast-moving water below. The sheer volume of water passing below the bridge each second was intimidating in itself. As the thunderous noise made it impossible for us to hear each other speak, we had to shout. The speed of the water - so close to us - made your head spin.

Gwen was clearly terrified by the prospect of having to cross the bridge. Perversely, this made me feel rather better about myself. Yet

I was worried for her. Surprised too as she - along with her partner John - had seemed the most relaxed and confident of our party up to now. John was quietly trying to dispel her fears. He pointed out that the heavily-laden dzos were waiting for us on the opposite bank and argued that if they could do it with all that weight to carry, then she too should be able to do it. Gwen didn't seem convinced though and gradually John started to become a little irritated with her as his efforts to persuade and coax her all failed. Our guide Vivienne and some of the other women in the group then huddled around Gwen and tried reassuring her in gentle tones. I could see that their words and calm attitude were starting to have an effect. Just then, unfortunately, up strode our big boisterous companion Richard, impatient to get going. 'Come on Gwen!' he said. 'There's nothing to it. I'll give you a piggy back if you like.' John gave Richard a look that suggested this wasn't the best way to handle the situation and Gwen turned to hide her face against John's chest. But Richard, who was beginning to strike me as perhaps not the wisest of men, stayed where he was, scratching his head in perplexity.

Eventually, John decided to take a more urgent tone and told Gwen firmly that she must cross the bridge and that there was no choice about this if they were to see Everest. When he pointed out that it would ruin everyone else's chances too, she seemed to respond to his words and started to summon up her courage. I knew there were several other bridges to cross before we reached the main Sherpa village of Namche Bazaar but decided to keep this information to myself for the time being. Selfishly I really wanted Gwen to cross the bridge so that our outward trek would not be interrupted. Eventually she agreed that she would cross the bridge if she were allowed to go first and if she could have John immediately behind her. Vivienne agreed at once. Gwen now walked over to the bridge and took a first tentative step onto it as we all watched and followed.

When my turn came to step onto the bridge, I was initially surprised at how firm it felt. Because of the missing planks though, I was forced to look down to carefully watch where I was putting my feet. It was impossible in these circumstances to escape the feeling of giddiness as I saw the rush and heard the roar of the water below. It was truly terrifying and the feeling threatened to overwhelm me. So I decided to hold on more tightly to the ropes and keep looking straight ahead, feeling for the gaps between the boards with my feet and proceeding very slowly towards the opposite bank. Many of the boards were wet and very slippery. Luckily the ropes felt very secure. I would probably have preferred to tackle the bridge a little faster but Gwen set a very slow pace.

When we were all safely across, Gwen suddenly announced with a smile of relief, 'That was fun!' We all looked at each other. Gwen continued to smile. 'I told you it would be easy' said Richard cheerfully. 'I'm looking forward to crossing it again on the way back.' Gwen's smile immediately disappeared. John glared at Richard who didn't notice. He was busily looking around for something.

'Oh bugger!' he said. 'I've left my rucksack on the other side.'

---

By mid-afternoon we reached the spot where we will be camping this evening. We're on the edge of a tiny hamlet which has a wayside tea house where we will be eating our evening meal. So we'll be indoors. This isn't going to be a regular occurrence apparently. We have a large communal tent which we will be using once we get further into the mountains.

The dzos, the porters and some of the Sherpas had arrived before us and I was impressed to see that our expedition tents had already been set up for us. These people work fast and are eager to please us by making life as easy and as comfortable as possible. Some of the porters were still busy unloading the dzos who, once they'd been relieved of their burdens, wandered over at a leisurely pace to a nearby branch river which was flowing gently through the wide, open side valley we had now reached. The large communal table had also already been set up and a table cloth laid over it. The table was spread. Foldable wooden chairs had been set up for us and it felt as though there was actually precious little for us to achieve for ourselves other than deposit our day sacks in our tents, where even the groundsheets, sleeping bags and pillows had been laid out ready for us. Our main rucksacks were there too.

We all sat at the table and there was a general sense of relief that we had managed to get through our first day. Much of the talk as we took our tea, which was delivered by two female Sherpas who smiled genially and uttered the words 'Tea, coffee?' questioningly, was of the river crossing and the condition of the bridge. Gwen was the subject of much admiration and congratulation which I think she was actually finding a bit irksome, though she smiled gratefully and graciously.

As we relaxed and unwound, some of the Sherpas were busy making our evening meal. Others were sitting or squatting, no doubt glad to be relieved of their heavy baskets. They smoked and talked amongst themselves, I noticed. This little scene on the banks of this gently flowing river set the pattern for how things will be organised throughout the rest of our journey in the mountains, a pattern which leaves us Westerners free to concentrate on walking while the support team does all the heavy work and makes all the preparations. We are at leisure to take in the scenery and enjoy the sheer experience of being here.

We all have a light day sack for our cameras, sun cream and the odd item of clothing, mainly ones to protect ourselves from the sun. We've all read - and been reminded by Vivienne - of the harmful effects of sunlight at this altitude. During the day, even when it's cloudy, we're all wearing dark glasses with side protectors and also white hats and white scarves too to cover our necks. You get sunburn more easily at this altitude and you need to keep your skin covered. It's another example - as with the water - of the need to be vigilant at all times.

Local people, intending to be kind, offer us water as we pass their doors but we have to refuse which seems ungrateful or discourteous, even insulting possibly. Some invite us into their homes but once more we have to refuse their hospitality. This makes me rather sad. It feels like a good opportunity missed. To a linguist like me it feels all the worse that we can only signal our refusal with our hands or by shaking our heads. We can't even extend them the basic courtesy of turning them down in their own language.

Vivienne warns us that we will have to be even more vigilant with regard to protecting our skin the higher we climb, especially when we reach the snow line as the snow will reflect the sun's rays back onto us. By that time too we will be better acclimatized and able to walk further each day, she says, so we will be exposed to the sun's rays for longer. It hasn't yet become second nature to me to remember all of this and I find myself removing my white hat from time to time and even my sunglasses. Then I catch Vivienne's eye.

There's one tent set well apart from the rest and it has a jolly-looking flag waving in the gentle breeze. No separate loos for the ladies and gentlemen here. I do notice, however, that it's for the exclusive use of us Westerners. I look around but can't actually see another tent. Perhaps the support team have different arrangements. But then, I'm struggling to find any of their tents at the moment and am not sure where they'll be spending the night. Anyway, our toilet tent is at a suitable distance from the rest of the camp and affords the appropriate amount of privacy. It even has a sign to show when it's occupied. Perhaps I half expected to find old newspapers inside but then remembered that there are no printing presses in this part of the world. It was much easier for the expedition organisers to pack proper loo paper for us. And what do you know? It's soft paper.

Our evening meal passes uneventfully. I think our party are all a little jaded by now. It's been a very eventful few days for us and we're all looking forward to a good night's rest. Vivienne advises us during our evening briefing over our post-prandial coffee - or tea in my case - that we need to be up bright and early in order to make the most of the daylight hours. There's a groan but Vivienne then points out that as it is dark outside and as there is no night-time entertainment available locally anyway, we may as well catch up on some sleep and get into the habit early on of going to bed as soon as it gets dark.

Tomorrow, Vivienne continues, we'll be making our way slowly to the village of Namche Bazaar, a name which conjures up as many mysterious associations and images as the name Kathmandu does. We're to walk at a funereal pace, especially during the last strenuous uphill section to Namche. We don't need to move as a single group and we can stop to rest as often as we feel the need to, but we should always keep the rest of the party in sight. Today we've lost quite a bit of height on our walk from Lukla and yet we all struggled with our breathing at times. Tomorrow's walk promises to be a hard one as we haven't yet acclimatized. However, once we get to Namche, Vivienne concludes, we can look forward to taking two days to relax and acclimatize.

# Tuesday 28 September

At 7.00 our morning cuppa arrives. Talk about luxury! Peter opens the flap of our tent and there are two of the female Sherpas standing immediately outside. I recognise them as the pair who served us yesterday afternoon. My eyes linger briefly on one of them who strikes me as pretty. Each of them is holding an enormous teapot, one with tea and the other with coffee. I think the only words of English these two kind women know are 'Tea, coffee?' And they have a perpetual smile.

Then they leave us to wake up a little with our morning drinks and return in a quarter of an hour or so with a bowl of hot water for each of us so that we can wash discreetly in our tent. As a matter of fact, though, this was my second wash of the morning.

I'd awoken very early and had got up a long time before the rest of our group. Peter was still asleep in his sleeping bag when I unzipped the tent door. It was astonishingly cold outside and I had to put on my coat, hat and gloves. I went for a solitary walk along the bank of the river to enjoy the morning atmosphere and the countryside around me while the porters and Sherpas were busy making our breakfast, erecting the communal table and starting to pack away their own belongings. I was soon away from them. I enjoy moments like this on my own. For someone who walks the mountains alone quite often, the peace and beauty of the countryside are important. However, I didn't like to wander far from the camp and within an hour or so - having washed my hair, my feet and my face in the freezing water of the river, just for the fun and exhilaration of it - back I came, invigorated, to the camp. There was no sign of any of our group and so I returned to our tent and lay on my sleeping bag.

It had rained hard during the night. This was not a good omen as far as I was concerned. The monsoon season is obviously not quite over yet and we can only hope that it will come to an end soon. The thought of walking in the rain doesn't really appeal to me. But worse than that is the thought that we might not be able to see the mountains from Namche Bazaar where we should be high enough to get our first distant glimpse of Everest and her close companions, Lhotse and Nuptse.

At breakfast there are frequent references to the weather. Clearly I'm not the only one who is concerned. Spirits seem a little low this morning and it's difficult to tell whether this is because people have just spent their first night under canvas at altitude or because there's a distinct chill in the air or whether it's just normal morning sluggishness. Or maybe there are other reasons, including perhaps the prospect of a longish day at altitude with the ever-present discomforts of being unacclimatized. It's wearying not to be able to breathe comfortably and perform at your best. Even turning over suddenly in bed last night made my heart beat fast.

As we eat at our big communal table in the open air, wearing our coats and woolly hats, I glance from time to time at the porters - busy as ever - starting to take down their tents and load our heavy packs onto the backs of the dzos. We're still drinking our third cup of the morning - they like to make sure we take plenty of liquid on board as it helps with acclimatization - when the first of the dzos are sent on their way. The local people treat them with great respect and look after them well, I've noticed. I don't actually know whether they are revered more for religious reasons or because they play such an important part in life here as beasts of burden. They're certainly indispensable to us. Without them we would have had to employ a small army of porters.

The temperature rises by a few degrees and with this warmth comes a general improvement in our mood. Woolly hats are replaced by sun hats, sun cream is applied and protective scarves are wrapped around necks. Vivienne reminds us yet again of the importance of keeping all parts of our bodies covered either with items of clothing or with cream. Eventually, people start to drift away to their tents to make their final preparations before setting off on our first full day's walk. We're not expected to do anything other than pack away into our main rucksacks anything which is to be carried onwards to the next camp and also pack our day sacks. The rest is left to our Sherpas and porters who, without delay, start to fold up our sleeping bags and ground sheets, dismantle the tents and neatly arrange all the goods ready to be packed and loaded.

---

By about eight o'clock we were all ready to leave camp. It was cloudy but there was no sign of rain. We ambled along in the direction of the river and awaited Vivienne's instructions. It was a gentle start to the day for us. Initially we followed the right bank of the Dudh Khosi river in the direction of Namche along a well-worn path. Soon however, the path became more uneven as it meandered through areas of large white stones and boulders. Though the sun wasn't shining, we were all aware that stones such as these reflect the harmful ultra-violet rays we were protecting ourselves from. The general line of our advance was still clear enough, not least because we could see a chain of dzos in the distance and at this point all we had to do was follow them.

After a quarter of an hour or so our leg muscles started to warm up and people seemed generally more cheerful and positive than they had been at times during breakfast. Just ahead, the ground to our left started to steepen, eventually giving way to a near vertical face eroded by the river. It was clear that we would soon need to cross to the opposite bank once again. I found myself looking for a way over the river but for a while I could see no obvious route. Then, from among the huge boulders ahead, a bridge appeared. I could hardly believe my eyes and found myself looking around to see the reactions of the others as, one by one, they realised what lay ahead. If yesterday's bridge had given us pause for thought, this one created a confusion of impressions and feelings - mostly not good ones. Fear, for sure, was in there somewhere. At the same time there was something comical about the bridge's appearance. It made you want to exclaim, 'Surely you're joking!'

The bridge looked little better than a Jenga tower after it has just collapsed into a pile at the end of the game. These collapses usually make the players laugh. However, this was no laughing matter. For one thing, the bridge was very low to the water which was pounding against it and shaking it. The creaking was audible even from a distance. To say that the bridge was crude of manufacture would be seriously to understate the case. Basically, it was in three sections of almost equal length. Each section consisted of a few thick planks of wood laid lengthways at right angles to the river bank and tied together. The section nearest to us had been lowered to a point considerably less than half way across the river and was secured to the bank by ropes tied around boulders. A similar section had been constructed on the opposite bank using the same method. These two sections each sloped upwards at quite an angle. They jutted out towards the middle of the river but were not quite long enough to meet above the water. So a third section had been built. This third section had been balanced on top of the highest points of the other two sections and tied to them with rope. The news filtered through to us from the Sherpas that it was a temporary bridge as the old one was swept away a fortnight ago.

Perhaps the flight from Kathmandu with its dramatic landing at Lukla, coupled with yesterday's precarious bridge crossing and the wearying effects of lack of oxygen, were beginning to take their toll. But I reasoned to myself that as the dzos had obviously managed to cross this ramshackle bridge then it should really present no problem to me, even if it did wobble visibly. I instinctively looked at Gwen. We all did. But she seemed not to notice that she'd become the focus of our attention. She hesitated, as the rest of the group had, but then walked boldly ahead of us to the bridge, turned and said sternly to Richard, 'Whatever you do, don't leave your rucksack behind this time!' With that, she clambered onto the bridge and climbed up to the far end of the sloping first section where she then had to step up onto the level middle section. She proceeded gingerly along this on her hands and knees and I watched, impressed, as she then stood up and stepped carefully down on to the final section which sloped down towards the far bank. In no time at all, it seemed, she was waving at us from across the river and inviting us to hurry up. She had made it all look very easy which it wasn't by any means. It required good balance, a firm nerve and careful placing of the feet as all the planks were wet and slippery and as water was continually being sprayed over our boots and trousers. I was amazed at the contrast between the Gwen of yesterday and the one I had just witnessed. Richard seemed rather lost for words. He was the last to cross today and remembered his rucksack of course.

---

We have lunch on the riverbank at about midday. The bridge notwithstanding, it has been quite an easy morning. I've been feeling strong and would have been quite happy to carry on. But I assume our guides know what they're doing. Acclimatization is a gradual process and it's important not to overtax yourself. At every opportunity, Vivienne coaxes us to drink more water to help the process or at least to prevent us from dehydrating.

Once again, the porters had arrived at our lunch spot long before we did and everything was ready for us. As usual, we were welcomed warmly by the two Sherpa women with the large teapots. As the water has been boiled it is quite safe to drink. We enjoy a leisurely lunch followed by quite a long break. We all seem to be getting on well by this time. Everyone knows everyone else in our group and the conversation is relaxed. There's laughter now and then. As I look about me I realise that there are still possibly a couple of people I'm a little unsure about or perhaps I sense that they're a little unsure about me. Maybe it's because they know I write books and are wondering what I might write about them! But even in a group of just fifteen it's common for smaller sub-groups to form. Peter and I always seem to gravitate towards each other, certainly, though we both mix readily with all the rest too. All in all I think we're quite a happy bunch. Except Elaine perhaps.

As the porters finally start to clear things away, Vivienne takes the opportunity to give us a gentle word of warning. The gist of it is that she wants us to walk as slowly as possible this afternoon in order to give ourselves the best possible opportunity to get used to the lack of oxygen in the air. As I'm feeling fine at the moment, I don't think I quite attach the significance I should to her words. Nonetheless, being an obedient sort of chap - I was the sort of boy who always did as he was told in school and at home - I set off at a snail's pace with Peter at my side. We carry on the conversation we had been having about Bill Forsyth's excellent film 'Local Hero' and Mark Knopfler's wonderful music for the film. Peter and I share a love of Scotland. Like me he knows the Munros and Corbetts well and we're having great fun comparing experiences of visits to places such as Torridon, Skye and the Cairngorms. It's a good feeling to be able to discuss these familiar mountain areas with him, particularly so far away from home.

The effects of the lack of oxygen in the air start to become clear to me as soon as we reach the long climb towards Namche Bazaar. It isn't that the ground is particularly steep. Anywhere else I would be striding forth but here I find myself stopping every hundred yards or so to catch my breath. It's slightly embarrassing for an experienced mountain walker but everyone is finding this climb hard. The hill seems to go on forever as I grow more and more tired. This shortage of oxygen - which comes over at the time as a shortness of breath - is a strange sensation. There's plenty of strength in my legs - and there's plenty of determination in me of course - but I feel a little as I used to feel in my karate classes when my training partner, during one particular exercise, had looped his belt around my waist and, standing behind me, was doing his utmost to prevent me from walking away from him. Or perhaps it's as if you've suddenly put on a couple of extra stones in weight. Your body simply won't do what you would normally expect it to and it can leave you feeling very frustrated. At the same time, your heart has to work much harder than normal. You can hear it pumping away in your chest.

It seems a very long afternoon, an afternoon of walking very slowly with frequent stops to rest. Conversation between us has almost dried up as it is so difficult to talk except when we stand still. But at about five o' clock, there are signs that we are reaching the outskirts of Namche. The sight of an occasional building is very welcome. My confidence about my fitness at lunchtime has gone by now and I'm having serious doubts about whether I will acclimatize well after all. It's consoling to see that everyone else seems to be finding the going hard too.

At the same time it's rather galling to see that one of our number, George from Lincolnshire, who is a rather heavy smoker, seems to be doing as well as me. Adding to my slight annoyance is the fact that he doesn't have the appearance of a fit man, shall we say, and that he once told us at dinner that he has a sedentary job and had never been for a hill walk in his life until a couple of weeks before coming out here to the Himalaya when, he thought, he should do a little preparation.

Hmm. We're all different. Peter though is able to tell me that it seems that smoking can help with adapting to high altitude because smokers' lungs have been used to working with less oxygen. Just the same, we're both determined to reach Namche before our unfit companion.

At length we do arrive at Namche - ahead of George - and our path widens slightly into a track. At the side of the track we reach a little old lady who is selling trinkets which she has on display on a low wall. There are carved animals, little bells and a variety of bracelets, necklaces and lucky charms. I spot one particular trinket which I know will appeal to my mother. It weighs very little and I can already see it on my parents' mantelpiece with the rest of the odds and ends I've brought back from my travels in other countries. I buy a bracelet for Jane too. Unsurprisingly, the lovely old lady speaks no English but I learn somehow that she is from Tibet. We barter, which seems to be obligatory, and throughout the process she talks non-stop. She appears well satisfied with the price we fix on. With her permission I take a photograph of her while she's negotiating her next sale with John and Gwen.

Namche Bazaar is perched in a natural amphitheatre high above a narrow and deep valley. The scenery here is simply magnificent. All around are high mountains, some just high enough to have permanent snow, and for the first time we begin to feel that we've made real progress on our trek, though Everest and the highest peaks are still some way off. Our little camp is near the upper end of the village, outside one of the many tea houses, and from here we get an amazing and panoramic view of the magnificent topography of the Khumbu region, as it's called. Or perhaps I should say that we get occasional glimpses of it, for the clouds of the late monsoon are still about. Perhaps for this reason it's the colourful houses of Namche itself, lying in the scooped out half-bowl of the hillside, that the eye keeps returning to. Namche is the ideal place for an adventurous spirit. Safe, cosy but very far from the big wide world outside.

Namche is often referred to as the capital of the Sherpa country. It's certainly the main trading centre and hub for the Khumbu region. People come here from the surrounding villages to the market, as they have been doing for centuries. Throughout the ages it's been a trading post for people from over the border in Tibet too. The Sherpa people themselves, in fact, have historic links with both sides of the border. What beats me is how they were ever able to climb over the high snow-covered passes with their wares. I think of our little old lady on the edge of the village.

More importantly perhaps, from an economic point of view, Namche is now without doubt the focal point for anyone who is on their way to the high mountains in the Everest region. It's the gateway to the mountains and is understandably popular with trekkers. As a result, the village has an air of relative prosperity. The houses are big and many are splendid in appearance, having been whitewashed and painted in a variety of bright colours. There are several permanent shops here too and some of them sell clothes, goods and equipment for climbers and walkers. Much of it is second hand - gear left by climbing and walking expeditions over the years who didn't want to carry it all back to Lukla.

In the meantime Peter and I briefly visit our tent which has been erected, with all the other tents, before our arrival by our support team as usual. They have chosen an area of flat ground right next to the main track through the village. Once we've left our day bags in our tents we join the others in the tea room for our post-walk afternoon tea. I soon realise that a number of my fellow-travellers are complaining of headaches. This is a sure sign of lack of oxygen in the blood. The other common signs include loss of appetite, lethargy and low spirits. It's as well that we're due to remain here in Namche for two nights as this will improve our chances of acclimatizing. At the moment, I'm feeling perfectly fine. In fact I feel great. As soon as we stopped walking the shortness of breath left me and I've been able to appreciate and relish the fantastic scenery. I try not to make too much of my feelings though. Peter is keeping quiet too. Peter the secret doctor.

Perhaps the sight of so many people with symptoms of mild altitude sickness reminds him of his professional skills, not that there's anything he can actually do to treat them. At this point I remember that I've read in several books and articles that those individuals who struggle at the outset often acclimatize best over time. Perhaps I too have problems ahead.

Unfortunately it's still cloudy and there's no sign that the monsoon season is coming to an end. But Lakpa seems convinced that there's a change ahead. He's really looking forward, he says, to being able to give us our first distant glimpse of Everest tomorrow morning. His plan is to take us to the top of the ridge behind the village where we should be able to see the high mountains for the first time. This will form part of our acclimatization too, a short walk to a higher point and then a descent as we return to Namche. 'Walk high, sleep low' is the phrase you often hear used by mountaineers. Tomorrow though will mainly be an opportunity to relax and let our bodies get used to the conditions at altitude.

I quiz Vivienne about the famous Everest View Hotel which was built just a short distance away by a consortium of businessmen from Japan and also about visiting the nearby villages where the Sir Edmund Hillary Foundation has built schools. Vivienne says she hopes there will be time to visit these places on our way back from Base Camp but shows little real enthusiasm for the idea. I feel rather disappointed at this. I've been looking forward to seeing these places for myself as I've read so much about Ed Hillary and the wonderful achievements of the Foundation. He was very keen to put something back into the region - and indeed the country - which made him world-famous.

# Wednesday 29 September

Today has been an interesting and varied day to say the least. A lot has happened on what I feared might be an uneventful - and possibly tedious - rest day. But I've found Namche Bazaar a fascinating village and I've had an enjoyable day here. That said, I still have worries about the weather and also about acclimatization. And about Peter too.

I don't think Peter slept well last night and I'm becoming increasingly concerned about him. Even though he can be very good company and we have plenty to talk about in our sleeping bags before sleep - music, travel, work, the environment and politics - the impression I get at times is that something quite big is troubling him. He won't talk about it though. I've certainly given him opportunities. I'm walking that tightrope between friendly inquisitiveness and interfering. As a doctor, of course, he's used to secrecy and confidentiality. Perhaps his professional approach makes it difficult for him to confide in others. I'm aware that Vivienne has spotted that all is not well. More than once she has been up to him during the last couple of days to ask how things are. She asks us all, naturally, as she needs to check how we're acclimatizing, but a glance she gave me at one point yesterday, just after she had spoken to Peter, suggested to me that she too has concerns about him.

But to go back to the start of day. Morning tea arrives. I poke my head out of the tent and see at once that the weather hasn't improved at all. If anything it's worse today. Even though the village is quite visible, there's low cloud above us and I can't even see the ridges above the village and certainly not the mountains which surround us. There's no way that Lakpa is going to be able to show us Everest this morning as he had hoped. I smile and thank the two women Sherpas courteously of course. But inside I feel disappointment.

After breakfast, where Peter declares that he's going back to bed, I head off on my own with my camera. First, as if to make my own disappointment worse, I climb to the top of the ridge behind Namche and look in the direction where I know Everest lies. There's nothing to be seen. At this moment I can't help feeling that this has been a long way to travel - and a lot of money to pay - just to walk in mist. I can hardly expect a thick mist like this to clear in the course of today.

I drop a little in the direction of Namche which soon comes back into view below me. The village is clear of mist and I decide to wander around the upper part of this natural amphitheatre I'm in and take a number of pictures of this striking and unusual place and of some of its inhabitants too. At one point I spot an old woman tending her vegetable garden below me. I watch her as she used a hoe to turn the top soil. She is poor but colourfully dressed, like so many of the local people. I wonder how old she can be and I suppose I'm surprised to see someone so elderly doing such hard work. She works away diligently and with great patience it seems to me. With my zoom lens I'm able to take photos from a distance. This way she remains unaware of me and I don't intrude on her privacy. Of course, I could have gone down to her garden and asked her permission but there are several terraces between us and no obvious direct route to her. Besides I want to pursue my way, deep in thought, to the end of the terrace I'm standing on and onwards to the edge of the village.

A few minutes later the old woman puts down her hoe and for a moment I think she's going to turn towards me and perhaps see what I'm up to. Instead she merely picks up an implement which looks to me like an adze. I've never seen an adze in use in my life, except of course the adze on an ice axe which, I suppose, should really be called an ice adze because of the position of the cutting edge relative to the shaft. In any case, in my mind an adze is a primitive tool and I watch the old lady in fascination as she uses it to break up large or perhaps hard clods of earth.

Further down in the village I take a photo of a local man who - though it is still only midday - is completely drunk and hardly able to walk let alone do it in a straight line. I take his photo from behind for some reason. I can't avoid him though as I have to walk past him. I give him a wide berth. I'm probably hoping he won't notice me but he does and, as drunkards back home or anywhere else for that matter often do, he greets me. The old fellow bellows something incomprehensible at me as I walk by. I pick up my pace.

When I get home to Britain I intend to give slide shows to raise money for charity and characters like this will add a human dimension to the story of my trip to Base Camp and beyond. I'm particularly fond of the photos I took - with the mother's permission - of a baby in a wicker cradle which she was rocking on the stone floor outside her home near Lukla when we were there. Word has reached us too that the former Duchess of York, Sarah Ferguson, is heading our way on a separate trek. Though I'm no royalist I will be keeping my eyes open for her as photographs of royalty still seem to make an impression. More importantly, in my eyes anyway, I'm looking forward to catching up with the climbers who are going to make an attempt on the summit of Everest. Among the international climbing team is the actor Brian Blessed who has been invited along by the expedition organisers. I'm keen to see him again, not least because he's partly responsible for me being here.

My gentle stroll around Namche, taking in the scenery, taking a handful of photographs and just reflecting on things - as I'm given to doing - lasted about three hours in all. I was now drawing near to our camp and could feel myself getting ready to be amongst people again. I pass some of the Sherpas first and am greeted with smiles and 'Hello', which I return. Some of the porters are sitting on their haunches, smoking and chatting amongst themselves. I pass various members of our group and make my way to the tent I share with Peter. He's not there. I take a drink, write some notes in my diary and then stretch out on my sleeping bag. It's a rest day and there's little to do. It feels like Sundays used to be back home during the time when it was still considered the day of rest and you sometimes got bored. In those days there was hardly anything open on Sundays except the churches and chapels.

After a while Peter appears and I'm glad to see him. He asks me about the village and about the photographs I've taken. He's very chatty and no longer appears preoccupied or worried. We wander outside and exchange words with some of the others. Most are sitting or lying about, talking and drinking tea. Vivienne is on the prowl and she tells us to be sure to take on plenty of fluids. I obey of course. I'm happy to drink tea at any time.

I spot Lakpa on his own and say to Peter 'Let's go and have a chat with him.' I'm hoping Lakpa will agree to have his photograph taken and he's actually standing by a whitewashed wall which will make an excellent background. Also, I've yet to have a good, long chat with him. So over we go, Peter and I, to say hello and try to discover more about our main guide who has already been to the summit of Everest twice.

Like the other locals he has a ready smile and strikes you immediately as a modest, humble type. He's small in stature and rather wiry in appearance. I find myself wondering how on earth he was able to get himself up Everest. On the other hand I've seen him helping with the packing and loading from time to time and I know he's a man of enormous physical strength in spite of his appearance. He's also a natural leader and good organiser. He has to deal with all the other Sherpas and the porters and it's his responsibility, ultimately, to make sure that the expedition runs smoothly.

During the course of our conversation we learn that Lakpa is from one of the nearby villages in the Khumbu region. He tells us in his broken English that he has been taking part in expeditions since his early teens and that as a child he had always wanted to go up Everest.

Impressively he has been up several of the other high mountains in the Khumbu region including Cho Oyu, a magnificent mountain which is the sixth highest in the world and another therefore of the world's fourteen peaks over 8,000 metres, so coveted by mountaineers everywhere. I have to stand back and pause as I try again to reconcile his achievements to his size. Lakpa is true mountaineering royalty. Yet he's so unassuming. I ask him hesitantly whether he will pose for a photograph for me. 'Of course,' he says, smiling. Luckily I had noticed during our conversation that he had a logo from one of his Everest expeditions on the back of his tee shirt. Thinking this would add to my photo I ask him would he mind wearing his tee shirt back to front for me. 'Of course,' he says once more, immediately taking it off, turning it around and putting it back on again. I take his photo and so does Peter.

I came away from that encounter with Lakpa inspired. It was as if his experience radiated from him and warmed me through, like a microwave oven. My negative thoughts about whether I'd be able to acclimatize and even my concerns about the weather seemed to dissipate and I felt a new confidence. To me, this was a huge adventure. To Lakpa this was surely just a gentle plod, something very comfortably within his range of ability. I told myself to draw on his strength.

Peter and I then return to our tent, passing some of the Sherpa women on the way. Once inside the tent Peter suddenly says 'Madhu seems to have taken quite a shine to you'. 'Who's Madhu?' I ask, a little disingenuously as I guess who he's referring to, though it was true that I didn't actually know her name. 'She's the tea-coffee woman - well, one of them - as if you didn't know!' I smile. 'Well, perhaps she realises I'm Welsh,' I say to him, unable to think of anything more sensible to say in reply. In truth I feel a little uncomfortable about the possibility that there may be speculation about me and this Madhu, attractive though she undoubtedly is.

All of a sudden we could hear the laughter and talk of children just outside. So out we went. Standing on a hillock right behind our camping spot was a small troupe of schoolchildren in their blue and white uniforms, looking smart and tidy. They were all smiling at us and shouting 'Sweets'. This is a word they've learned from other visitors from the West who had brought sweets to make friends with local children. The result, of course, was that the children's teeth were spoiled in no time and dental care isn't easy to come by in this remote part of the world. This has changed to some extent since the Sir Edmund Hillary Foundation built a hospital in one of the nearby villages but the hospital relies entirely on doctors from the West who come here to work temporarily and they have limited equipment and drugs. Their hours are limited too.

I had read before leaving Britain that children would ask for presents and many of us had brought useful things to give them rather than sweets. I'd brought a couple of boxes of blue biros which they could use in their school, also built by the Sir Edmund Hillary Foundation. The biros were obviously most acceptable. The children flocked around me to receive their gifts. Some of the children then ran off delighted with their spoils but others lingered to try and carry on a conversation with us in their own language and to examine us, strange beings that we were. For some reason I felt slightly envious of them. Perhaps because they were growing up in a place of such overwhelming beauty. Or maybe simply because they were so young and full of joy.

It isn't that life here is easy for them. These small children walk over three miles to school in the next village every morning and that village is a good deal higher up than Namche. At the end of the school day they then have to walk another three miles home again, obviously. It's impossible not to consider how easy life is for schoolchildren back home. I remember my mother telling me that she used to walk several miles to school with her friends when she was a little girl living in rural west Wales. It's no wonder the little children of Namche are so tough and healthy-looking despite the poverty in Nepal. Also, they're able to cover these distances without their parents and feel completely safe. This is certainly food for thought.

The porters were beginning to gather together a short distance away and I got the impression that something was afoot. I knew they had been watching us engaging with the children. My view of the porters so far is that in essence they're rather shy, unassuming, humble people and stand somewhat in awe of us. Just then Lakpa crossed to us and said that some of the porters would like to meet us. I think we were all glad of the opportunity to further break the ice even though the language barrier makes it a near hopeless business. All the same, we had lots of fun trying to get through to them. We all stood around smiling at each other but quite unable to converse in any meaningful way, of course. This complete failure, though, only made us all laugh. Laughter at least is international.

It was obvious that we held a great deal of fascination for the porters and fortunately I'd brought with me from home some photos of myself and Jane and also a few photos of our garden and of the countryside around our home. These proved very popular and were examined closely before being passed around. A number of porters asked Lakpa to translate the questions they had for me about local flowers and birds as well as about cars and the size of the house I lived in. They seemed to assume that I lived in the mountains and when I told them that the highest mountains in Britain were just over 1000 metres they all laughed. Their curiosity at seeing photographs of a far-off country was truly surprising. I couldn't help wondering what they made of it all - this country they would almost certainly never see for themselves.

Gradually the small crowd of porters started to drift away and they returned to their tasks. Peter and I went back to our tent to see whether the clothes we'd washed that morning had dried. Then we walked down to the village together once more. I'd seen one or two shops which were selling mountaineering clothes and equipment and Peter was keen to see what was on offer. We walked into a shop right in the middle of Namche. It took a while for our eyes to grow accustomed to the darkness inside. Then we could see wooden shelves reaching up to the ceiling and all covered in a confusion of goods. In the corner was a pile of oxygen bottles which it seemed had been left there by a team of climbers from Italy. On one shelf I found an old purple water bottle. I checked that the opening was wide enough for my purpose and that the lid - which was on a short chain - fitted tightly. All was in order so I bought it. But not for carrying water. It will come in handy on the cold nights ahead when I'm tucked up in my sleeping bag and don't want to venture out of the tent!

When we came out of the shop the fog over the village had cleared and the sky was blue. The sudden transformation surprised and delighted us. It was rather like emerging from an afternoon showing of a film at the cinema. We skipped back to the camp as Lakpa had mentioned possibly going for a short stroll up to the ridge behind the village if the weather were to improve and we certainly didn't want to miss this opportunity to spend time with him, learn from him and maybe get to see Everest for the first time as well, albeit from a distance. This, after all, is why I've travelled all this way and for all I knew this might be my only opportunity.

As luck would have it, we got back to camp just as Lakpa was about to set off with some of our group - those who felt strong or well enough to walk. We learnt that a few were still suffering from persistent headaches or simply felt too tired to move. Some were off their food. I felt relieved to be feeling fine still - for the moment, at least. Phil, Mark and some of the others who were complaining of headaches yesterday were all looking better today and decided to join our party. I noticed that Elaine, who has shown no symptoms of altitude sickness so far, didn't accompany Phil.

We set off for the ridge behind Namche where I'd walked this morning in thick mist. None of us though had acclimatized enough to be able to climb the short pull which leads from the campsite to the ridge without immediately feeling out of breath. By the time we eventually reached the ridge there was no doubt in our minds that the weather had improved greatly. Lakpa had been right to say that the weather was about to change. The heavy clouds associated with the monsoon - the unbroken blanket of grey - had finally gone and now the sky above our heads was entirely blue except for a few high white clouds here and there.

Lakpa pointed in the direction of Everest where it was a rather different story though. All we could see over there was a covering of white cloud. We stood watching for a while and every now and again we caught very short-lived glimpses of a snow-covered ridge. But as quickly as it came into view it disappeared again. Gradually I gained the impression that each glimpse was starting to last slightly longer than the previous one. But perhaps this was wishful thinking. I was feeling increasingly excited but also increasingly frustrated. Were we now at last going to get a clear look, however brief, of Everest itself? As the minutes went by and we all watched in hope and silence, the veil of white cloud parted and closed again several times more. There was definitely a ridge top to be seen at times. But this was not Everest according to Lakpa. From here, the mountain called Nuptse stands between us and Everest. If the cloud were to clear altogether we would be able to see the uppermost part of Everest behind Nuptse's long ridge, he informed us.

We stood there for another quarter of an hour hoping the cloud would clear completely. Some were getting cold and were stamping their feet and rubbing their gloved hands together. Time after time, the cloud started to lift but then closed again and hid everything once more. This teasing continued up to the point where most of us were starting to talk of calling it a day. But still we lingered, unwilling to give up. Then, gradually but definitely, the clouds finally started to clear altogether. The hole slowly grew larger and larger. It was as if someone - determined to tease us for as long as possible - was softly drawing back the curtains to unveil a masterpiece. And, at last, there it was. Everest, the highest mountain on Earth! Five and a half miles high, the equivalent of nearly nine Snowdons piled one on top of the other. This is why we have come all the way here. To see with our own eyes this graceful, enormous mountain which made such an impact on the imagination of people in the twentieth century - and not just climbers. As I stood looking at Everest whose summit was peeping out over Nuptse's long ridge, I recalled the famous words of Mallory when he was asked by a reporter why he wanted to reach the summit of Everest - "Because it's there." I didn't want to take my eyes off the mountain I'd read and heard so much about and which was now little more than a few miles away. But I made myself reach for my camera to take a number of photographs before quickly putting it away so that I could gaze on Everest again.

I remained transfixed for a while but eventually Lakpa told us our dinner would be ready before long and that we would need to set off back to the camp. With some reluctance, I turned my head away and set off with the rest of the gang, though I couldn't resist looking back over my shoulder several times until we reached the point where we were too low down to see Everest.

By the time we reached the village once more and put our belongings in our tents, night was slowly drawing in. Not long afterwards, at the dinner table, all those who had been up to the ridge and seen Everest were talking enthusiastically about their experience. If the others were jealous or sorry that they hadn't joined us, they kept it to themselves. As a matter of fact everyone was in a good mood, even those who earlier had shown mild symptoms of altitude sickness. The rest day has done us all good, we're all starting to acclimatize and the weather has improved too. Things look promising this evening and I'm feeling elated.

Whatever happens now, I can at least say that I've seen Everest with my own eyes, albeit from a distance of several miles. And tomorrow we should reach the famous monastery at Tengboche, one of the highest monasteries in the world and certainly the one with the most spectacular setting, surrounded as it is by some of the world's highest peaks.

# Thursday 30 September

Today was another day of walking very slowly - at a funereal pace - through stunning scenery. We're now well and truly on our way towards the high mountains. Most of our morning walk was easy as we made our way along a level ridge well above the valley floor. It's a strange feeling to be in the quiet back country once again after two days in Namche with its town atmosphere. Now, once more, we find ourselves on our own and with only few signs of habitation.

The day had started as usual. I've a feeling I kept eye contact with Madhu to a minimum this morning when she appeared with her companion bearing our hot morning drinks. Over-sensitively and incorrectly I'm sure, I felt that Peter's eyes were upon me at this point. When the two Sherpas returned a quarter of an hour later with our bowls of hot water for our morning wash inside our tent, I noticed that Madhu gave her bowl to Peter today. My morning brain was running away with me and I was wondering whether she, like me, had been quizzed or teased by a companion about an imaginary connection between the two of us.

Long before we had awoken properly and got ourselves ready for the day ahead, the porters had as usual prepared breakfast for us and as we sat to eat it they immediately started the daily job of storing away everything that was no longer needed in an orderly manner, ready to be loaded onto the yaks. Yes, from here on it's the shaggy black yaks who will be carrying our worldly goods. Yaks are better adapted to high altitude than the dzos which are a cross with a domestic breed of cow. They are easily distinguished from the dzos who have been accompanying us up to now. It's their long black hair which is their most obvious feature. They're generally placid creatures but as they have enormous horns on their large, powerful heads we've been warned to be careful not to stand too close to them in case, for example, they turn their heads and accidentally knock us off the narrow paths and down into the gorge.

I decided at once always to allow a yak to pass if I saw one just behind me. It soon became second nature to keep looking over my shoulder.

Towards midday we find ourselves losing height. Ahead we can see that the yaks have stopped. This is a sure sign that it's almost lunch time and that our morning's work will soon be over. As we draw near, the women with the teapots are already moving towards us, even before we sit down. Our cups are presented to us and filled at once. I wonder whether this is a sign that we won't be staying here long. But it's nothing of the kind. This proves to be the most leisurely lunch we have taken so far on our adventure. We spend the time sitting in a small walled field high above the valley but with a view ahead which foretells a hard walk in the afternoon. We can see a broad track climbing steeply through a tree-covered hillside. Vivienne tells us that at the top of this hill stands the monastery at Tengboche.

Tengboche! The very name evokes images of black and white photos and footage of the British expeditions to Everest following the Second World War when Tibet was closed to foreigners and Nepal was suddenly opened up, at least to the British, who were able to use their long-established imperial connections and influence in this part of the world. In my mind's eye I see black and white images of these remarkable monks welcoming and blessing the white climbers from the West who had their minds set - oddly as it must have seemed to them - on reaching the summit of Chomolungma, The Mother Goddess of the World. I see the scenes as the climbers were introduced to the head of the monastery, who welcomed them, blessed them and placed a white scarf around the neck of each one. These early mountaineers were sensitive to the feelings of the monks and local people, and realised the importance of Everest both in their view of the world and in their traditions. It would be a privilege for our group to be welcomed into the monastery but foreigners are not normally allowed within its walls these days.

Even if we were fortunate enough to be able to visit the monastery, we wouldn't be walking on the same floorboards as those early mountaineers. And even the monastery visited by them was not actually the original one. In fact it was relatively new at the time of the post-war expeditions. In 1934 the monastery was destroyed during an earthquake and subsequently rebuilt. However, it was destroyed once more by a fire in 1989. The story goes that electricity had been installed in the building by well-wishing Americans. One of the elderly monks, believing that the way to turn off his new electric fire was to turn it face downwards, caused the old wooden monastery to be burned to the ground. Most of the monastery's priceless collection of old documents, as well as its statues, murals and wood carvings, were destroyed, though some books and paintings were salvaged by trekkers. The monastery was again re-built, however, with money donated from several countries and with help from local people and an international team of volunteers. This is the current building which we will see later this afternoon, all being well.

John Hunt, leader of the British Expedition to Everest in 1953, thought Tengboche one of the most beautiful places in the world. 'The Monastery buildings stand upon a knoll at the end of a big spur, which is flung out across the direct axis of the Imja river. Surrounded by satellite dwellings, all quaintly constructed and oddly mediaeval in appearance, it provides a grandstand beyond comparison for the finest mountain scenery that I have ever seen, whether in the Himalaya or elsewhere.' I'm impatient to get there.

Peter was very chatty this morning as we walked along together. He talked a good deal about the surgery where he works and the various pressures there are on him both as a doctor and in particular as one of the partners in the practice. By now, especially by means of our increasingly open and relaxed nocturnal chats in our sleeping bags, I feel as though I know his wife and children quite well. I know their names, their interests and something of their different personalities. It's odd to think that we were complete strangers, Peter and I, until about a week ago.

This afternoon, then, following this very restful lunch, we start on the very slow climb through the wood towards Tengboche. I happen to be walking close to Lakpa at one point and we fall into conversation. I learn from him that we're going to be camping near the monastery. I'm delighted to hear this and want to ask him more. But I realise he has his duties to attend to and I'm keen not to detain him for any length. However he seems happy to amble alongside me and chat, and in the event I actually spent quite a bit of time talking to him this afternoon.

One reads frequently that the Sherpas are modest, quiet and self-effacing and this is certainly true of Lakpa. Heaven knows he has plenty he could blow his own trumpet about! He tells me that he hopes to go on his third ascent of Everest next year with an expedition from Switzerland. In his broken English this likeable man talks to me quite openly about his family, his plans and his aspirations. He tells me which village he is from but the name doesn't mean anything to me at the moment. While I'm talking to him about the 1953 British Expedition he mentions once more that he is related to Tenzing Norgay. Hearing this I feel a connection - albeit a very distant one indeed - with the mountain and its history. He's such an amiable man and I'm sorry I'm not able to speak to him in his own language. He does like his cigarettes though. He's been smoking all afternoon as we Westerners struggled uphill to the monastery at Tengboche. We keep talking until I start to feel that I really must save my energy as the uphill walk is becoming a bit of a battle for me. He shoots off ahead as I pause once more to draw breath.

It's a long and very tiring afternoon. The lack of oxygen in the air affects us all. It's a relief rather than a delight to reach camp at Tengboche. The Sherpa women greet us cheerfully as ever but it's hard to force a smile or even observe common politeness when you feel so wiped out. The general mood isn't helped by the fact that we're now enveloped in low cloud once again. There isn't a single mountain in view let alone the splendid panorama containing what John Hunt described as the finest mountain scenery he had ever seen. In fact we can barely see the upper parts of the monastery as we pass it on our way into camp. What an anti-climax this is for us all. To say there's a mood of despondency in camp at the moment would be to understate the case.

Rest and a drink are remarkably reviving though and soon the conversation picks up once more and takes on more positive and hopeful tones. Perhaps it will clear up soon, we tell each other. Perhaps the monsoon will come to an end as Lakpa - and he should know, shouldn't he? - has been telling us for the last two or three days.

Vivienne is going around the group smiling and chivvying us along and generally doing her best to be reassuring. She tells us to rest in our tents and take on more water. There's even time for an hour's sleep before dinner if we want it, she says. It certainly isn't long before most of us head for our tents. What a blessing that we didn't have to erect them ourselves after such a hard walk.

In our little tent, Peter is clearly of the view that the only option is to be optimistic. His is a reasoned, logical approach. No matter what we may currently feel about our prospects for acclimatizing properly or for seeing Everest close up, it's important in his view to retain a positive outlook and not be overwhelmed or misled by the effects of fatigue at the end of a tiring day. Moods change, he states, but whether or not the monsoon is going to come to an end has nothing to do with our feelings. In essence I agree with him but usually prefer to work through my moods and allow them to make their impressions rather than chase them away or dismiss them in this way. Peter settles down to read. I take a nap.

It's dark by the time Peter and I make our way to the communal tent for our evening meal. We take our headtorches. Inside, though, we can turn them off as the kerosene lanterns brighten up the atmosphere and give off their familiar smell. Most have arrived before us and I'm glad to see that people seem relaxed and that the conversation is flowing. It occurs to me too that everyone is getting along well. Just at this moment we seem like one happy family. Even Elaine is smiling. Throughout our meal there's laughter. Some are talking of back home and of how they came to decide to come on the expedition. A number of us had hesitant family members to contend with. Some had to resort to subterfuge. One member says he had considered pretending to be a doctor so that he could come along at half price and a discussion followed as to how he might have been found out in the event of a crisis. I catch Peter's eye.

This is exactly the kind of atmosphere in which Richard thrives. He is at his most chatty and communicative - and entertaining, to be fair.

He tells us in his loud voice of the difficulties he faced persuading his employer to release him for the expedition at what was a busy time for the company and he recalls some of the ruses he had dreamt up. Laughing, he tells us of the expensive meal, on a short break in London, during which he informed his girlfriend that he had signed up for the expedition. He clearly felt her response had been unreasonable and the whole saga, as he related it, was very entertaining. Perhaps it didn't actually register with Richard that his audience was probably more in sympathy with his abandoned girlfriend than with him but his very amusing way of telling us his story probably provided just the tonic our group needed this evening.

The tables were being cleared and, driven on by his success, Richard now produced a pack of cards. We remained there in the tent for at least another hour and a half playing games we all knew. Laughter filled the tent from time to time and Vivienne - taking advantage of our good mood - kept forcing more and more water on us. At length, fatigue and sleepiness started to get the upper hand and the merriment gradually subsided. The meeting eventually broke up and we all left the communal tent more or less at the same time.

Outside we were stopped in our tracks. The mist had completely disappeared. Our eyes were drawn upwards to the night sky. With no lights to spoil the view, it seemed that we could see thousands and thousands of stars perfectly clearly. It was by far the best view of the northern sky that I had ever had. The monastery, which was no more than a hundred metres or so away to our left, was in silhouette I noticed. But to our right, still a few miles away as the crow flies, we could just make out Everest's snow-covered summit catching what little light there was. It was wonderful to see it again and I was delighted for those who hadn't climbed with us onto the ridge behind Namche yesterday. In the silence of the late evening Everest seemed to be calling to us and the last words we exchanged before the cold of the night air gripped us and drove us to our beds were full of hope, anticipation and excitement.

Of course, there are still three days to go before we reach Gorak Shep, the last settlement of any kind on our route, and another two days on top of that before we reach Everest Base Camp. Gorak Shep stands on the glacial moraine at about 17,000 feet in an area of extensive rock and ice which has virtually no vegetation. It isn't inhabited all year round as the months of winter mean it becomes unbearably cold there and it can be cut off by snowfall. At this altitude, few trekkers feel comfortable and many start to suffer symptoms of altitude sickness or acute mountain sickness. It's a bleak place by all accounts but this is where we will pitch camp before climbing the mountain called Kala Pattar. Its summit gives the best view of nearby Everest which is hidden from view when you're at Base Camp. Of course, there's no guarantee that all of us will actually make it to Gorak Shep or be in any state to enjoy the experience if we do make it. For tonight, though, I'm going to share Peter's optimism. A good rest, a good meal, a good laugh and a clear view of the heavens have completely changed my mood as I pull on my woolly hat and get into my sleeping bag. The nights are now very cold.

# Friday 1 October

This morning, the sun is shining and the sky is blue and clear. Now, for the first time, we see for ourselves why so many say that the views from Tengboche are among the finest in the world. From the flat and extensive top of the mountain where we now stand - a plateau really - there are high mountains in every direction, and all covered in snow. A stupendous 360 degree panorama. We're looking at some of the highest mountains in the world. This includes the unusual looking Ama Dablam, which is as memorable and unique in appearance as the Matterhorn. We stand transfixed as we gaze on the magnificent, breathtaking scenery. This is definitely what we came here for. I turn slowly on the spot, naming the mountains I can see - Kwangde (6187 metres), Everest (8848 metres), Nuptse (7855 metres), Lhotse (8616 metres), Ama Dablam (6856 metres), Kantega (6679 metres) and Thamserku (6608 metres) to name but a few.

Because it's such a fine, mild morning, the porters have erected our breakfast table outdoors. This means we can have breakfast looking at Everest. It raises its head above the ridge of Nuptse which still stands between us and the bulk of Everest. We can see that thin wisp of cloud so often to be seen at its summit, like a plume of light smoke. The trouble is that it's difficult to sit down for long or to concentrate on eating. People stand to take photos or gawp at the scenery before sitting momentarily to take another mouthful.

Views such as this one do a great deal to raise the spirits of tired walkers who have been on the march in difficult conditions for several days, especially when there have been lingering doubts about whether you'll get to see the mountains at all. So we're all feeling pretty inspired and ready to face another day on the move. I certainly am.

By the time we finish our breakfast, the first yaks have been sent on their way and the ever-busy porters and Sherpas have, as usual, got most of our equipment stored and ready for carrying. The porters are busy loading the last of the larger items onto the few remaining yaks before they turn their attention to loading the huge wicker baskets they will be carrying on their backs. No-one is exempt. Even our charming cook, Dawa, who is only a little over five feet tall, has an enormous load to carry including pots and pans which dangle at his side. The baskets have a belt or strap which they tie not around their wastes but around their foreheads. When walking, they stoop forward slightly and their eyes are on the ground. They will take the weight off their heads and necks by holding onto the strap with both hands unless one hand is needed to carry the stick which they use to prop up their baskets when they pause, as they must from time to time, to rest.

In the meantime, we make a final visit to our tents to gather a few things together and get ready for the day's walk. I look up and see Lakpa walking towards us from the direction of the monastery. Before long he is standing among us and announcing that we have been invited into the monastery by the head monk. There's a real buzz among us when we hear this news. We listen carefully as Lakpa, with a little help from Vivienne, briefly tells us what to expect and explains a few matters of etiquette.

Within a few minutes we were entering the courtyard outside the main entrance to the monastery itself. Some of the novices were busy sweeping and doing other domestic chores but each one stopped to greet us with a smile, a slight bow and a stock phrase of welcome. We were escorted by a more senior monk towards the main entrance, where the doors were opened to receive us. Inside we were introduced to the head monk who welcomed us in words we couldn't understand. He spoke for several minutes and we listened in silence while Lakpa did his best to translate his words. The head monk ended his greeting by extending us his best wishes for a safe journey. At this point we were presented to him one at a time and we lowered our heads to receive the traditional gift of a white scarf and his personal blessing. With this, our audience with the head monk came to an end.

We were by now all itching to take photographs of the inside of the monastery before setting off on our walk. Lakpa explained that we were welcome to take as many photos as we wished, though not of the monks themselves. For some reason, I'm having a few difficulties with my camera today. As this is the only camera I have here, I'm more than a little concerned. All my photos of the expedition so far are on it. I fiddle with the settings and hope for the best. Luckily there are one or two in our group who are really good with cameras and I pick their brains.

The journey towards Everest from Tengboche starts downhill and, inspired perhaps by the good wishes from the head monk and also by the excellent views and weather, we walk more quickly than usual and make good progress. In spite of the lack of oxygen at this altitude we all feel much better walking downhill. But once the ground levels out again - and especially when we come to any sort of uphill pull, no matter how slight - you're reminded immediately how difficult it is to walk when your body isn't fully acclimatized. That said, most people seem to be coping better today. Those who have been complaining of headaches over recent days are now reporting that they feel well again and everyone seems to be in good spirits. Myself included. I'm excited at the prospect of seeing Everest close up and am also feeling refreshed and full of energy following a good night's sleep.

During the morning our journey is through countryside which is comparatively green and fertile. It's pleasant on the eye. As we make our way along the track, Everest disappears from view for a while only to reappear as we reach the top of a rise. With every new rise it's getting ever closer and seems to loom larger. My excitement grows with each new view. The mood is a good one as we take our lunch. But by mid-afternoon things have changed, especially for me perhaps as I become aware of a new kind of lethargy which is beginning to grip me. I feel the beginnings of a headache and walking is becoming harder. I can tell that my mood is changing too. And so does the landscape around me.

We're now in a region which is entirely different in appearance to that we witnessed this morning. Around me it is bleak. There isn't a bush or a blade of grass to be seen. All seems arid, stony and grey. The barren world around our feet is in sharp contrast to the magnificence of the high mountains around us, their summits and upper reaches covered as they are in permanent snow. My eyes are constantly drawn upwards to gaze at them, especially magnificent Ama Dablam which now dominates the view. I'm aware that the sight of the mountains is still inspiring but I begin to feel that I'm looking at them now to distract myself, as if the mere act will make my headache go away. But it doesn't.

I feel dog-tired by the time we reach the tiny settlement of Pheriche which lies in the middle of a wide, rocky valley. The village itself does little to lift my spirits. It seems squalid and grimy to me at the moment. It has an air of poverty and a shabby look about it. All the buildings are of wood and look run-down. Perhaps I'm looking for a little comfort but I can see at once that I'm not going to get it here. Everything I see reflects my own dismal feelings as my headache unquestionably grows worse. And we're due to be here in this forsaken place for two days, it seems.

We've now climbed to a position which is considerably higher than where we were this morning. As I begin to feel the effects of altitude I recall - as if to torment myself - the way I was feeling just a few hours ago when we emerged from our tents to see the sunshine and the glorious mountains and again later as we left the monastery, blessed and inspired.

Peter knows there's something wrong but he also knows there's absolutely nothing he can do about it. If I fail to adapt to the lack of oxygen during the next forty eight hours I face the prospect of having to go back in the direction of Tengboche and perhaps further. The only cure for the symptoms of oxygen deprivation is to lose altitude and return to where the air is not as thin. I've been dreading this moment and am now seriously worried that I won't be able to reach Everest Base Camp. At the same time, feeling wretched as I do, I'm not sure I want to do anything other than go home. Home is where you want to be when you feel ill or when you need to recover. But home is now many, many days away.

In camp we follow the normal routine. Tea arrives straight away. I think I detect a look of sympathy in Madhu's face as she pours mine. But it may be all in my mind. Perhaps it's just me projecting my wishes onto the world outside because I'm feeling sorry for myself. Still, she seems to linger longer than is strictly necessary and for as long as she is able before duty calls her away with her companion to the next little group.

Vivienne, ever vigilant, is soon at my side and encouraging me to drink plenty of water. She suggests that I try to take a nap in our tent before our evening meal. She's really emphasising the need to keep drinking and also to rest. Perversely I resent her attention and advice, which is silly. But I'm starting to feel that I want to be left alone and my mood dips a little further. I wander over to the tent and find Peter already asleep. I'm relieved that I don't need to talk and stretch quietly out on top of my own sleeping bag. It's dark inside the tent and I'm soon away in the land of dreams.

I can never sleep for a long time during the day. A late afternoon nap of twenty minutes or so seems to be my limit. During these naps I always feel as if I'm only just below the surface of consciousness and that I'm still at least half aware of sounds around me. At the same time, though, my naps always seem to be full of dreams. Today I'm dreaming of being in discomfort. Suddenly it isn't me that's in discomfort but someone else. I hear a groan just as I wake up.

But it isn't Peter. In fact Peter is no longer in the tent with me. I'm feeling refreshed. I'm even feeling a little better as my headache has subsided. I suddenly want to be amongst people and don't want to miss what little daylight remains for today. So I leave the tent. Almost at once I hear not a groan but the sound of crying from one of the other tents. I'm aware that people are standing around expectantly. Richard comes over and starts talking to me in subdued tones. He tells me that one of our group, Terry from Yorkshire, had reported to Vivienne that his wife, Pauline, was complaining of stomach pains. He then asks me whether I knew that I'd been sharing a tent with a doctor. Thinking there was a tone of accusation in his voice I mutter something extremely vague but Richard interrupts, telling me that Peter had leapt into action when he heard about Pauline's pain.

Pauline's pain came on suddenly it seems. I'm surprised, almost shocked. She has been the picture of health and I know she's among the fittest in our group, a person who takes walking holidays all over the world and who, back home, runs six miles a day. She is a cheerful soul too. Always smiling, always happy apparently. She's one of those people whose company is a tonic, particularly if you're feeling a little low for any reason. To say she has a positive outlook on life is an enormous understatement. To think that Pauline, of all people, should be unable to cope with the altitude or with anything else is really disconcerting for me at this particular moment. I realise for the first time that, in fact, throughout the last week or so I've been drawing on her strength myself. We probably all have and now she's been laid low.

I watch Peter as he emerges from Pauline and Terry's tent wearing his professional face. I find myself admiring him enormously. To have those skills! To have that ability to tend to the sick! Of course everyone is looking at him inquiringly and Peter is avoiding eye contact with the gathering crowd. They want to know how Pauline is. I think there's a little confusion mixed into their reaction too. I can almost sense them adjusting their perceptions of Peter to include the idea that actually he's a medical man - not a dustman at all. I knew he had wanted to keep quiet about his true professional identity and I felt a little sorry for him because of the awkward explanations he would now have to give. He paused to speak with Vivienne before walking towards me outside our tent. He went inside and I followed him. To my inquiry about Pauline he gave only a general answer of course but I noted the look of concern on his face.

Later though, when we assembled in the group tent for our evening meal, I spotted Terry laughing away with Richard and some of the others. I took this to be a good sign and when Pauline arrived a few minutes later she had her usual cheerful smile on her face and greeted everyone in her customary, friendly way. Perhaps she was a little more subdued than normal at times, I thought, but clearly she was no longer in pain. During dinner, there were questions from concerned friends - which we all were by this point in our adventure - and she spoke quite openly about the sudden attack she had had and the attention and reassurances she had received from Peter. I remembered the look of concern I had seen on Peter's face when he returned to our tent but it was clear now that it couldn't have been for Pauline's welfare. In the meantime he waved away the thanks he was getting from the group and especially from Vivienne for acting so swiftly and he also dealt as well as he could with the occasional flippant remark about dustbins and waste collection policy.

I was feeling a little better myself this evening and was glad to be amongst people rather than on my own. Just the same, I was hardly in party mood. Annoyingly, Richard has adjusted to the altitude rather better than most of us and he talked and behaved boisterously throughout the meal. He has a knack of catching the general mood of the group - though sometimes getting it wrong - and adjusting the volume and frequency of his comments accordingly. He had picked up on the general sense of relief that Pauline was now better and he was in celebratory mood.

At one point, Vivienne was doing her standard act of urging us to drink more water. Instead Richard produced from a bag a large bottle of whiskey. To his credit - for he's a generous and well-meaning man at heart - he immediately offered it around to everyone in the group. Vivienne was in despair but couldn't make herself heard above the laughter and comments provoked by the sudden appearance of the bottle. Everyone sensibly refused Richard's offer as alcohol will only hinder our acclimatization. Nothing daunted, he poured a little into his coffee and then announced loudly that he was off to the toilet before retiring for the evening. He added rather too much detail and then headed outside.

Following a slight pause in the conversation inside the tent, a few tentative remarks were offered about Richard. More people then came forward with their own views. There seemed to be general agreement that, in his favour, he was undoubtedly generous and gregarious. It was agreed too that the presence on an expedition of outgoing individuals such as Richard was good for keeping up morale. At this juncture, someone mentioned the sleeping arrangements. As there's an odd number of us, one of us has a tent to himself. This, until today, has been a fellow called Jonathan but it seems he has consented to an appeal from Jason, who has been sharing with Richard, to a change in the arrangements whereby Richard from now on will have a tent to himself. Snoring and flatulence were mentioned.

I was ready for my bed after a day which had started with a great deal of excitement but which became tiring and then slightly worrying. I didn't really enjoy my food this evening, another sign perhaps that I'm struggling to acclimatize, but my headache has stopped and I'm certainly feeling less rotten than I felt during the afternoon. Peter also looks tired and I'm relieved to find that he isn't in the mood to chat this evening as we normally do. Once in our sleeping bags we decide to get some sleep. Yet another early night. I'm certainly sleeping lots.

As I lie here the only thing on my mind now is my acclimatization. I just hope these are the worst symptoms I'm going to get and that I'm able to continue on the trek. I think there are only about four members of our group now - Peter included - who have shown no symptoms at all of oxygen deprivation other than being short of breath. One of our number, Jonathan, admitted to me tonight that he had considered staying at Tengboche because he was feeling nauseous as a result, he felt, of bad headaches. His confession came as a complete surprise as he has otherwise looked well to me. It would be an unbearable disappointment to me at this stage to be unable to get close to Everest, especially now that the weather seems to be settling into the familiar post-monsoon pattern with clear, sunny mornings and cloud gathering towards the end of the afternoon, followed then by very cold nights.

I drift off at some point only to be awoken by a strange sound coming from not far away. It seemed like the low, short cry of a bird. I couldn't recognise the bird and told myself that in any case I hadn't seen any birds since arriving at Pheriche. I raise myself onto my elbows so that I can hear more clearly. A minute of silence passes before I hear the cry again. Peter is now awake too. He asks what I think it might be. 'A bird of some sort,' I say, but he's concerned it might be a larger animal. 'Or the abominable snowman?' I add with a chuckle in an attempt to relieve any real anxiety he may have.

Temple in the Kathmandu valley

Monk with begging bowl

Street scene in Kathmandu

Girl in Lukla

The benevolent Buddha watches over you

Our plane leaves us behind in Lukla

Temporary bridge over the Dudh Khosi river

Lakpa who had been up Everest twice

Breakfast outside Tengboche monastery

A wobbly bridge with several planks missing

Even the cook had a heavy load to carry

Wayside Mani stones with devotional designs

Namche Bazaar, the Sherpa capital

Yaks and a boy who wants to be in the picture

Tibetan woman with her wares

Our first glimpse of the summit of Everest peeping over Nuptse's ridge

Looking back towards Ama Dablam

The Duchess of York and her guides in Namche

Standing on Kala Pattar before the cloud cleared

Everest (left) and Lhotse

Looking down at Base Camp, the Icefall and over the pass into Tibet

Standing at the foot of the Icefall

The author and Brian Blessed, Kathmandu airport

We hear the sound again and then all is silence once more. In the course of the next few minutes, though, the sound becomes gradually more frequent and grows steadily louder too. Being still half asleep and gripped by a certain amount of concern for our safety, it took a while for it to dawn on me that I might actually be listening to a human voice. A female human. As the cries became louder still and very frequent, all doubt as to their cause was eventually removed from our minds. 'I suspect it's Pauline we're hearing,' said Peter. By this time I felt sure that everyone in camp must have been awoken by the cries and I could imagine all our companions lying there in their tents and listening with great interest. It was all highly entertaining.

'This always reminds of "In the Hall of the Mountain King," I say to Peter as the cries reach a crescendo. Peter guffaws at my remark and has to put his hand over his mouth for fear of being heard by Pauline and Terry.

Once the heights of passion had been reached, Peter and I settle down once more to sleep. Next morning, at breakfast, we all politely greet each other with 'Good morning' in the usual manner. I'm grateful that no-one asked me whether I'd slept well or made remarks about a peaceful night's sleep and so forth. Pauline and Terry are munching away heartily. I'm rather hoping that Pauline will offer no apology for keeping us all awake. She shows no sign of embarrassment, however, and so I focus on my breakfast.

'I slept really well last night,' said Pauline suddenly. Silence threatened to engulf us and so someone made a comment about the weather and the subject was taken up hastily by several of us. The huge tent flap opened and in came Richard, last to arrive as ever. He sat down next to me and an uncomfortable feeling ran through me. Richard looked across the table at Pauline. 'That was quite a show you put on for us last night,' he blurted, stuffing a huge piece of bread into his mouth. Silence did engulf us this time. Richard didn't seem to notice however and merely reached across the table for more bread.

# Saturday 2 October

I'm writing this particular entry late in the afternoon as I look back on a day which has been no fun at all for me. Although I slept well - once I'd been allowed to, that is, by Pauline - I awoke with pain behind both eyes, as if I'd had far too much booze. I took the tablets I would normally take back home for a headache but they had no effect whatsoever. The pain wasn't too bad at breakfast and the goings on there kept me distracted. Afterwards though the pain grew gradually worse throughout the morning and by midday I was in a kind of daze and feeling thoroughly wretched. The situation was made more difficult by the knowledge that there was no prospect of losing any height today and thus get more oxygen on board. At least we're not moving to a higher camp as this is a rest and acclimatization day for us.

To make matters worse I've lost my appetite altogether. I didn't even go to the communal tent for lunch and I certainly shan't be going for dinner this evening. Not only did I not want food by lunchtime but I didn't want to see anyone either. In this state it would be impossible to pretend to be cheerful and I certainly haven't been good company for Peter or for anyone else today. Every time I've seen her, Vivienne has told me to keep drinking water. Even when she catches my eye from a distance, which she seems to have done frequently, she makes a sign to me to drink. I pull out my water bottle obediently each time even though I hate the idea of swallowing anything.

Loss of appetite is a definite sign that my body is failing to adapt to the shortage of oxygen in the air at this altitude. There is nothing whatsoever that I or anyone else can do either to ease the pain or to restore my appetite. All I can do is hope that my body is somehow - without me knowing it or feeling any evidence of it - adapting while we're resting here in Pheriche. If I fail to adapt there will be no choice but to descend to somewhere where I can get more oxygen into my brain. To climb higher and ignore the symptoms is a sure way of inviting further problems and much more dangerous ones at that. I've read enough about acute mountain sickness and the horrors of pulmonary oedema and cerebral oedema and about deaths on the mountain to know that it would be impossible to go on unless I acclimatize soon. Those conditions make for fascinating reading when they're happening to someone else in a book or an article but when you begin to suspect it might be happening to you yourself, it's a different matter altogether. It focuses the mind.

So I've been walking around the fringes of the camp like a zombie today and doing my best to avoid the company of others. I knew Vivienne was keeping an eye on me and determined to be out of view to her for a while I started wandering gradually further from the tents. At first I circled the site, moving from the area where our own tents were pitched and going beyond the nearby buildings to where the Sherpas and porters had their tents. Eventually I reached the edge of the village and would return to our own tents by a wide loop on the opposite side of the valley. Each circuit took me about a quarter of an hour. I was aware that I was just doing this to kill time and in the hope of distracting myself but it was quite impossible to ignore the constant pain in my head.

Every now and again I would pause to look around and, in particular, try and see our camp from a slightly different angle each time. In the distance I could usually see one or two of our group wandering about but I think most people were relaxing in their tents. The camp was a peaceful, still place.

I must on one of my circuits around the camp have taken a pause from my walk not far from where the Sherpas were, at the time, preparing dinner. I could smell the food being prepared. It smelt as good as ever but I knew also that I didn't want to eat even the smallest single morsel of it. At one point I was looking in the direction of our own tents in the distance. I had stopped to see the new view and perhaps to rest. I was leaning face-forward against a huge boulder when I became aware that someone was approaching me from behind. I turned. Madhu had broken away from the other women Sherpas and was now standing just a few feet from me. She smiled as usual but there was a look of concern on her face too. She said something to me. Of course I didn't understand a word. I forced a smile and shrugged my shoulders. She spoke again. Her tone was calm and I think she was trying to sympathize with me or reassure me. It was a private moment, just me and her. Fleeting. Then, just as quickly as she had appeared, she turned and walked back towards her companions who were busy about fifty metres away. I watched her as she went to rejoin them and I saw them turn to look at her as she approached them once more. There was giggling and I imagined that her brief talk with the Westerner had probably cost her some teasing. I'd been really moved by Madhu's brief display of sympathy but I was also sorry to think she might now be feeling embarrassed or that she was in an awkward position.

By now I had convinced myself that I had escaped Vivienne's vigilance and I decided to follow a natural ramp which climbed away from our campsite and onto a ridge overlooking Pheriche. I was drawn on too by the possibility that I might get a better view of the high mountains which were temporarily out of sight to us from our position in the valley. I had read about the stupendous view to be had from this ridge along one of the side valleys near Everest and didn't want to miss this opportunity. I had read too that a little walking could help the process of acclimatizing. They say as well that it's beneficial to sleep at a lower point than that to which you have climbed. So I trudged my weary way, lost in myself, along the gentle rise until I reached a point where I was walking on snow for the first time. It seemed soft enough and so I continued on my way, gaining height only very slowly. Soon I lost sight of Pheriche and found myself wondering whether I should now turn back. I passed a chorten, a wayside Buddhist shrine. I was on my own and no-one knew I was here. But I decided to press on regardless, drawn on by the idea that I would soon get a glimpse along the side valley whose entrance I could see about half a mile ahead. Ama Dablam lay directly ahead of me and was an excellent guide. Even so,

I felt that I was taking a risk and that if anything should happen to me now it would take a good while for me to be found.

However, I reached the entrance to the side valley and carried on a little way further until I could see along its full length. It was stupendous. There were huge snow-covered mountains on both sides and the whole valley was bathed in glorious sunshine. It was the stuff of dreams really, an empty valley which seemed as if it was completely unexplored. One mountain in particular looked close enough and tempting enough to make me pause. I've a feeling it was Island Peak, one of the highest trekking peaks in Nepal at over 20,000 feet. You need a permit to go onto its slopes even though it isn't technically difficult. It's a very popular objective because it's a relatively straightforward climb but it obviously still requires a good deal of stamina and skill. Experience with ice axe and crampons are deemed essential. Perhaps I even forgot my pain for a few moments as I looked at its inviting slopes which reached down in my direction. How easily I could have been drawn by such a view. But I realised that it would be madness to carry on towards it and I reminded myself that to do this might be to put our whole adventure in jeopardy. I took some photos, took a last longing look and turned back towards Pheriche.

As the crow flies, Everest is now no more than 7 miles away. From my current position on the ridge behind Pheriche, as I make my way slowly back to the village, I see Nuptse and Lhotse ahead of me. These are two of the giants among mountains and together with Everest these companion mountains form a horseshoe, rather like the Snowdon Horseshoe but many times higher and most vast, of course. I can't actually see anything of Everest at the moment but I sense its presence now. It feels so close. Its ridges and the Khumbu glacier which flows from the famous Western Cwm dominate the local topography. Everest is also the focal point for all human interest in the area these days.

A wave of excitement runs through me as I think of the adventures ahead, the things I have yet to see. More than anything I'm looking forward to the view of Everest from the summit of Kala Pattar, the hill on our side of the Khumbu Glacier which gives the best views of Everest. I'm also looking forward to the trek to Base Camp. To get there we need to walk on the Khumbu Glacier itself. This will certainly be the trickiest part of our journey. Glaciers are notoriously unreliable. Crevasses can open up suddenly. We will be utterly reliant on Lakpa and the other Sherpas to prepare a route through and along the glacier. It is likely to be a meandering, slow route as the safest line is unlikely to be a straight one. Unlike the glaciers in Europe, moreover, the glaciers here in the high Himalaya are covered in enormous, twisted towers of ice called seracs which look solid and formidable but which are known to collapse without warning. We can't avoid walking past them. They present a danger - albeit a beautiful one - that simply has to be faced.

At Base Camp we will catch up with the climbing expedition we're supposedly attached to. I can't really see in what way we're going to be of any use to them but it's a buzz to think that we are at least nominally attached to the biggest international expedition ever to attempt Everest. There are several mountaineers of some reputation in the team. One Uruguayan is hoping to become the oldest ever summiteer at the age of 60. But I'm more interested in Brian Blessed. I remember as a boy seeing him in 'Z Cars', an early black and white television police series made by the BBC and filmed live. I've also read a number of his books, one of which inspired me enough to make me consider a trip to Nepal. What sealed it for me was meeting Brian after a talk he gave in our local theatre during which he gave me a card with the name of the organisers of this, his second expedition to Everest. I was looking forward very much to meeting him again.

I was also looking forward to seeing the climbers from other expeditions. I hear Base Camp is something of a city of tents at the moment. Apart from the expedition we're attached to, there are currently climbing teams there from the United States, Japan and France amongst others. I know Base Camp is situated at the point where the Khumbu Glacier, after it tumbles from the Western Cwm in the crumpled and dangerous mess called the Khumbu Icefall, turns sharply to head down the valley. We'll be crossing the terminal moraine tomorrow on our way to Lobuche, the next settlement along our route.

When we return from Base Camp there will still be adventures ahead of us. Coming down from a mountain or returning from the high point of a trek can often be an anti-climax. Once the main business has been completed, it's tempting to feel that all you want to do is get home and to do it as quickly as possible. But when we return to Pheriche we will be turning into a different valley and heading upwards once more. This time we will be heading for a high pass called the Cho La which stands at nearly 18,000 feet and is covered in snow and ice most of the year. Once over into the next valley we will be away from the immediate vicinity of Everest and the scenery will be dominated by the exceptional Cho Oyu, another of the fourteen peaks in the world which are over 8,000 metres and regarded as the easiest of them to climb. We will then drop down this new valley and approach Namche Bazaar from a different direction, passing through other villages in the Khumbu region such as Khumjung and Khunde. If I get my wish, we will be visiting the Edmund Hillary School at Khumjung and on our way we will visit the famous - or notorious - Everest View Hotel. I'm looking forward to reaching Namche again. I might even treat myself to a beer once I get there. In the meantime though, I have to hope I get over this headache and acclimatize properly.

# Sunday 3 October

Following a rest day at Pheriche we might be expected to feel bright and perky. But the effects of altitude are now clearly starting to take their toll on our group and the mood in camp this morning was rather gloomy. Most of us are now feeling some of the effects of altitude. Nearly everyone - if not actually everyone - has by now complained of headaches, lethargy or troubled sleep and loss of appetite. People are listless and irritable. Even Richard is subdued. Elaine is strangely quiet. This is just as well since people are growing increasingly fed up with her perpetual moaning. I do feel some sympathy for her though and I've resisted joining in the complaining that goes on about her behind her back. I sense that she's no longer enjoying the trip.

One or two are trying to be positive and make encouraging remarks. Vivienne of course is doing her best to foster a positive approach. But it doesn't seem to be having much effect. Some are talking openly about missing home. One or two say they had no idea there would be so much discomfort involved in what was supposed to be a holiday. I choose not to get involved in this discussion. We were all warned about the effects of lack of oxygen. On the other hand, I suppose, it's certainly the case that we would have acclimatized better had we been given longer to adapt.

The day had started well enough for me, personally. Although I woke with a slight headache and although I'm slightly off my food still, I did at least sleep well. There are aspects of our daily routine which many have started to find tedious but I still find it cheering to be brought tea in our tent. It was good to see Madhu and her companion this morning too. I tried to smile a 'thank you' to Madhu for that moment of concern yesterday and watched her as she poured my tea. It's morning! We're still here! Everest is just around the corner! There's still so much to do and see and I'm damned if I'm going to give in after coming so far!

The walk this morning is once again, on the face of it, quite easy. The terrain is fairly level and the going underfoot straightforward. But it's the lack of oxygen in the air - or perhaps, more precisely, the fact that most of us haven't adapted properly to this lack of oxygen - which makes walking such hard work. Vivienne is encouraging us all to walk very slowly. Not that we have any choice actually. She moves up and down through the group talking to each of us in turn, almost forcing us to take on more and more water. But we're living on the edge. If only we could take more time to acclimatize the whole trip would be far more enjoyable. We pass walkers who are on their way down. Their cheerful smiles are in contrast to the almost permanent frowns most of our group are now wearing. Even at the very slow pace we're moving it's a real struggle to make progress.

There is a good lunch spot at Dughla on the way to Lobuche. We made ourselves as comfortable as we were able amongst the stones and settled down to eat - well, perhaps I should say to drink. I don't think anyone is feeling hungry and the food appears less and less appetizing as we gain height too. Even though we haven't walked far this morning, people are feeling tired and jaded. We're all glad to stop. Not least because Vivienne has intimated that this afternoon could be a little more trying for us. I have only to look ahead and see our path zigzagging along the terminal moraine to see that she has been understating the case. At this moment it looks prohibitively steep to me. It's all the more uninviting as everything now looks grey - a dirty kind of grey at that. The general impression at this height is that we've long left behind any vegetation and that we've moving amongst stones, stones and more stones in a barren landscape of unrelenting difficulty for humans. Unable to catch our breath fully or advance at anything like a normal rate, everything seems to suggest that we have no right to be here.

The afternoon begins. So does the steep climb up through the boulders of the glacier's terminal moraine to reach Lobuche. Everyone moves at a pace which reminds me of undertakers. Every hundred yards or so Peter and I have to stop to catch our breath. It's as if there's nothing in the air to breathe. No matter how slowly we move - and we are moving extremely slowly, more slowly than I've ever walked in my life - you just can't get away from the overwhelming sensation of breathlessness. People stop occasionally and slump over or lean against rocks in an effort to take the weight off their feet. The going is unrelentingly hard, our walk a debilitating slog. Fitness doesn't come into it. It's now simply a matter of whether our bodies can cope with the shortage of oxygen.

At long last, the ground starts to level out and we all heave an enormous sigh of relief - well, I do. Lobuche can't arrive soon enough as far as I'm concerned but there's still quite a long way to go before we can stop for the day. A long way ahead of us, in the distance, I can now see the last of the yaks as they plod steadily towards tonight's camp. It's little comfort to see them though really. For one thing, they're a good half mile ahead of us. For another, they're still on the move which suggests to my tired mind that we're nowhere near our camp. I find myself hoping that camp is just around the next corner.

Because we're no longer walking with our faces into a steep slope, I'm able to see ahead of us the mountain called Pumori. This means I'm looking over the border into Tibet. Even though I'm very weary I'm still thrilled by this. Pumori stands beyond the Lho La, the pass which was the Sherpas' traditional entry point into Nepal and the place from which Mallory himself first saw and named the Western Cwm. How exciting is that?! The peaks of Lingtren and Khumbutse also come into view as we proceed. The great flank of Nuptse still stands between us and Everest and behind us Ama Dablam continues to dominate. Tired I may be but the views are simply magnificent.

The route passes numerous memorial stones to Sherpas who have lost their lives helping Westerners to try and fulfil their mountaineering ambitions, mainly on Everest. It brings negative thoughts of the futility and blindness of personal ambition. I think of Jane, as I do every day. But I focus once again on my feet. With each tired step I remind myself that I'm getting a little closer to Everest and that the hard work for the day will soon be over and that I will then be able to rest. I see Vivienne approaching again and pause to take a drink of water. Though I've started to hate the taste, I know it's vital to keep taking on more liquid.

After an exhausting few hours, we finally arrive at Lobuche. It's a relief to get here and to be able to stop at last. It's still daylight and in spite of having tired limbs and a weary oxygen-deprived brain, I'm still able to be tremendously excited by what I see all around me. I'm now right in the thick of it all. I'm seeing with my own eyes that which I've only previously read about in books or seen in films and documentaries. Sitting outside our tent - already erected for us of course by the time we had arrived by our ever-reliable support team - I can feast my eyes on the Khumbu Glacier, Pumori, Kala Pattar, Nuptse and Lhotse. To my left is the Lho La. These are places I've dreamed of visiting. And now I'm here!

As the sun starts to go over, I sit and continue to take it all in. How wonderful to be able to sit still! I'm weary of moving, run down and fed up with not being able to catch my breath. We haven't actually travelled very far today but I feel as if I've done a full day's walk. Even the thought of having to unpack my day sack is draining, as is the thought of having to write my account of the day in my diary. I also feel slightly as if I'm in a dream, a little detached from reality and from my surroundings. It's a strange sensation and at times I catch myself wondering whether I really am here at all.

Lobuche itself is little more than a couple of lodges. It's too high and remote for permanent habitation. The winter snows make sure of that. This evening our temporary home is at almost 5000 metres. It promises to be very cold tonight. I'm sitting in sunshine at the moment and my superb duvet jacket keeps me warm. This only serves to remind me how cold it will become once the sun goes down, as it will soon. Once again I have a headache but it isn't as bad as it has been at times during the last few days. There are still two days to go before we climb Kala Pattar where, weather permitting, we will get our best view of Everest, the view I've seen in so many books. It's sobering to think that we still have another three days to go before we reach Base Camp.

# Monday 4 October

Our destination today is Gorak Shep. Before we set off I check my watch, not to see what time it is but to see how high we are. I know Gorak Shep to be at 5,160 metres and I'd like to keep an eye on progress today. But my fancy watch, which I bought in Singapore, has stopped recording the altitude at 4,444 metres.

I have a slight headache and my appetite is middling. These are the only symptoms I seem to have today and I find this encouraging. My determination is high too. I just pray that tomorrow morning the weather will be clear for our walk up Kala Pattar. It would be heartbreaking to have come this far - to have got this close - and yet fail to get the unsurpassed view of Everest and the Khumbu Icefall which is to be had from there. It's going to be hard work though as Kala Pattar stands at over 18,500 feet. Furthermore I gather we're going to have to make a very early start and that we'll be setting off in the dark. However to me - and for the rest of us, I imagine - this will be the climax of our trip.

Today's trek is to be a short one. We will be on the move for about three hours only. Vivienne says there will be plenty of breaks along the way too. This is all excellent news. We're especially delighted when Vivienne announces that we don't need to leave camp until eleven o' clock. I'm surprised Vivienne didn't mention this to us yesterday evening during her routine briefing. Perhaps she forgot. On the other hand, as the distance to Gorak Shep is not great I find myself wondering whether the itinerary has been altered in view of the general condition of the group.

Whatever the case, it's a relief to hear that we shan't be moving onwards and upwards just yet. We spend much of the morning sitting around in camp, talking and playing cards. The weather is glorious and we're able to sit outside in the sunshine. As I get involved in the game, my mind becomes more focused on the cards in my hand than on the stupendous scenery all around me. Then, from time to time, I look up and find myself thinking 'Oh look, there's Nuptse' or 'There's the Khumbu Glacier' and here I am - having made all this effort to get here in order to be able to see these wonderful sights - ignoring them and playing a mere game of cards!

But the morning wasn't all just cards. At the end of one particularly laughter-filled game Mark asked me if I'd like to join him for a stroll over to a couple of huge boulders we could see in the distance. He thought that from there we might get an even better view of the mountains straddling the border between Nepal and Tibet. I had my doubts but Mark turned out to be absolutely correct. Long before we reached the spot we were aiming for, I was kicking myself that I hadn't brought my camera. Because I was so tired, I had wanted to travel light and had decided to leave it in camp. However, as the views were once again fabulous I was happy just to take it all in and when we reached the two huge boulders we found a place to sit in silence for a while looking at the giant mountains. Mark was also able to take some photos as he'd shown more sense than me.

At length we decided to make our way slowly back to camp. As we strolled along we chatted about this and that. Mark is such an affable, mild-mannered chap. He's one of those people who it's hard to imagine anyone finding anything to dislike about. He speaks in calm tones, is a good listener who responds thoughtfully to whatever you say and I haven't heard him utter an unkind word about anyone throughout the time we've been here in Nepal.

Back at camp the extra hours of taking it easy and playing cards have made for a relaxed, even convivial, atmosphere. It's good to hear laughter and a little banter. Richard is busy trying to impress us with his witticisms. Our two London investment bankers, Gwen and John, are counting their winnings and are busy teasing the morning's biggest losers, who seem to be Pauline and Terry, though I think Jonathan may have been another. Vivienne is taking advantage of the good spirits to remind people of the need to keep drinking water at every opportunity. At this point Madhu and her companion arrive with the two enormous teapots which I now always associate with them. It's somehow hard to imagine these two charming women without them. As it was, I was very glad of a cup of tea following my stroll with Mark and thanked Madhu warmly for mine. I looked her straight in the eye as I did this.

'No fraternising with the natives, Andrews!' bellowed Richard suddenly from his position in the middle of the group. There was a little laughter and I felt distinctly uncomfortable. In these situations, always unable to think of the right response, I tend to feel that my silence only stands to confirm the idea which underlies the accusation. I probably smiled weakly as I tried to think of something suitable to say. But it was too late to respond and there was no option but to take it on the chin.

Everyone else's attention moved on immediately, of course, but the moment lingered with me. Then Peter came up to me and gave me a friendly pat on the back. He had a broad smile on his face and asked whether we should go and pack our day sacks so that the support team could start taking down the tents. Off we strolled together. He knows me well enough to feel he needs to remind me not to take any notice of Richard.

At shortly after eleven o' clock we have all convened at a point designated by Vivienne. Most of the group seem to be in a good mood still, though the thought of having to move once more after such a restful morning isn't particularly appealing. It certainly doesn't seem to appeal to Elaine. I remembered that I hadn't seen her during the morning. She wasn't playing cards or sitting about taking in the early sunshine with the rest of us. I felt sure I'd seen Phil at times though. Elaine was now slumped on a rock, motionless. All around her people were busy getting ready. Phil approached her from behind and put a hand on her shoulder. She shook it off. I decided to pretend I hadn't witnessed this.

Once you start walking and you realise that you're not actually going to be allowed to remain in the same place all day, you quickly adapt. It takes a while for tired muscles to warm up and it can take a little longer for your mind to adjust. But after all, we haven't come here to sit outside tents in Lobuche. I'm desperately keen to see those views from the summit of Kala Pattar and only a little less keen to see Base Camp with my own eyes and meet the climbers in the main expedition, as well as see Brian Blessed again.

On the subject of Base Camp, I happened to be passing Vivienne earlier when she was in conversation with Lakpa about the next few days of our trek. I only caught snippets though. They were talking quietly. However I heard enough to gather that they felt we ought not to spend two nights at Base Camp as our original itinerary had stated we would. On the one hand I was relieved that they weren't actually discussing leaving out a visit to Base Camp altogether. But I did wonder what had become of the idea of us doing a so-called 'environmental clean up' at Base Camp where so much detritus has accumulated over the years. It stated quite categorically in our literature that one aim of our trip was to contribute to such a clean up. Personally I wasn't keen on the idea of spending a day picking up litter at Base Camp, however much I care for the environment. I didn't believe the others would be keen either, given how hard we're still finding it to walk at altitude. I couldn't help thinking that some duplicity had been practised somewhere, perhaps as a way of gaining permission from the government of Nepal for such a large climbing expedition. The mess on Everest has certainly been the focus of media attention during the last year or so and the promise of a free clean up may have tempted the authorities here to grant the high number of climbing permits needed by the expedition organisers.

I soon put these matters to the back of my mind. I decide to discuss them with Peter this evening in the quiet of our tent. In the meantime it's back to the job of putting one foot in front of the other and getting myself to Gorak Shep. This in itself provides enough of a challenge to occupy me for the time being. The going is still very hard and I wonder why on earth it's taking me so long to acclimatize. Or maybe I'm acclimatizing just enough to be able to continue without any new symptoms or further discomfort. Whatever the case, the air feels thin and I find myself gulping it in and having to stop frequently to catch my breath. It's comforting to see that everyone else in the group is finding it just as difficult as I am.

As the yaks and our tents - already erected - come into view at Gorak Shep we can reflect on the fact that we've had spectacular scenery for every step of the way today. We have been rounding the end of Nuptse's ridge all day and more and more of Everest's flank has come into view as we've proceeded. Ahead still, we see the border mountains and we can also see into Tibet. This is inspiring, even for tired minds and legs. It's difficult to believe though, when you feel almost exhausted, that the day's walk has been such a short one and it seems laughable that we've only covered three miles in as many hours.

The evening drags and I'm truly impatient to get going up Kala Pattar tomorrow morning. Motivation is a fantastic thing. Tomorrow's mountain walk is the main reason I have come to Nepal. I have walked a long way and put up with a lot of discomfort simply to put myself in a position to be able to get that superb view of Everest from across the valley, the view I've seen in so many books. This is probably what made me stay on the hard bench at Gobowen station all those days ago.

During evening briefing Vivienne tells us that we will need to be up at 3am for the long walk uphill. There's a good deal of surprise at this, though no-one demurs at this point. As Vivienne points out, we can hit the hay this evening at 9pm or even 8pm if we wish and thereby get plenty of sleep. She also points out that there is hard work involved. She reminds us of the height gain and that the summit stands at over 18,500 feet. She adds that we should all feel confident about being able to do it as we're acclimatizing well and that in any case we will be spending a further night here in Gorak Shep so that the climb up the mountain is the only activity for the day. She takes the opportunity to slip in the information that we will only be spending one night at Base Camp. No-one objects. Finally she adds that anyone who wants to stay in camp tomorrow is free to do so. I, of course, am astonished to think that anyone would even consider missing the opportunity to go up Kala Pattar, which is the high point of our trip both literally and figuratively. But Elaine announces quietly that she will stay in camp tomorrow, adding that Phil however may go without her if he so chooses.

# Tuesday 5 October

So we were up at 3am. I was tired but quickly ready. Suddenly we're told that breakfast will actually be at 6.30. There were clouds down in the valley and therefore there was no hurry to get going, it was felt. But I was fired up. I was definitely not going to risk missing out on seeing Everest, no matter what. If the cloud were to clear, I wanted to be up there on the mountain and not down here in camp. Peter felt the same. We consulted Vivienne who agreed that Peter and I could skip breakfast and set off together ahead of the rest of the group. The extra time would give us our best chance of getting up the peak, we believed.

So, very early in the morning, Peter and I set off with our headtorches up the broad, clear path towards the first ridge on Kala Pattar. Our progress was very slow and we had to stop frequently to catch our breath. But determination can achieve a great deal. So can the realisation that you will only get one go at something. Gradually dawn broke and the time came when we no longer needed our headtorches. When it eventually became light enough we stopped from time to time to take photographs and to take in the stupendous panorama. The cloud below us had cleared and the view along the length of the Khumbu Glacier and Valley with Ama Dablam in the background was simply breathtaking. We congratulated ourselves on our decision to set off in the dark. It seemed it was certainly going to pay off, though there was still heavy cloud on Everest, Lhotse and Nuptse.

We were already quite high up on the mountain when we saw the others starting to make their way from camp. I looked at my watch and decided that they were either skipping breakfast too or that they'd taken it earlier than announced. I felt glad for them that they were likely to get good views on their way up. Though I was aware of a mild headache and pain behind one eye, I was otherwise feeling fine. I felt absolutely sure now that nothing short of a sudden medical emergency was going to prevent me from reaching the summit. It was a source of extra reassurance to know I had a doctor at my side.

Peter and I took plenty of time and lingered often to give the others a chance to catch up. This meant we could rest, take deep breaths, keep hydrated and have a bite to eat occasionally. We were too far ahead of the rest though for them ever to be able to quite catch us up. For us it was now just a case of moving slowly onwards and upwards. The heavy cloud across the valley was starting to lift and I felt increasingly confident that by the time we reached the summit I would get the view of Everest which I had wanted for so many years.

On we went until at length the summit came into view just ahead of us. The feeling of euphoria was overwhelming. By this time the cloud over Everest had dispersed altogether and we were basking in glorious sunshine. I realised now that despite all the worries I'd had about acclimatization and the weather, I was at last going to stand on the summit of Kala Pattar. Those worries - for all their effect on me - had actually come to nothing. Eventually, out of breath but happier than words can convey, we reached the summit. We shook hands and then hugged, patted each other on the back and let the sheer joy of it all - and the relief - do their work on us as we looked all around and took in the fantastic scenery.

Not long afterwards, as if from nowhere, Lakpa joined me and Peter on the summit. The three of us decided to walk a little way further along the level ridge ahead. Peter was flagging a little and Lakpa took his rucksack. Impressively, he carried this as well as his own much larger rucksack. And whenever Peter and I stopped to look around and catch our breath - which we did often - Lakpa would take out a packet of cigarettes and light up. Clearly this was a mere stroll in the park for him.

The weather couldn't possibly have worked out any better for us, either in terms of the views we were now getting or from the point of view of our climb which would have been even more tiring in the sunshine we now enjoyed. From the summit of Kala Pattar we had a superlative view of the bulk of Everest itself as well as nearby Lhotse and Nuptse. We could also just about make out the different coloured tents down at Base Camp, to the left of the great bend in the Khumbu Glacier. The Khumbu Icefall looked enormous and tremendously impressive, not to say intimidating, even from this distance. From our vantage point we could easily trace the route taken by climbers all the way from Base Camp to the summit of Everest. Once over the Khumbu Icefall they enter the Western Cwm. At the far end of the Cwm we could see the terrifying Lhotse Face and the way over, via the Geneva Spur, to the South Col of Everest. From there the ridge climbs steeply again to arrive at a relative flattening of the ridge at the South Summit. This was the point Charles Evans and Tom Bourdillon reached on 26 May 1953. To the naked eye, the distance from there to the main summit of Everest seems as nothing. They had just 300 feet to climb. They would have become household names had they continued and reached the summit. Instead, they turned back and three days later Hillary and Tenzing took the glory.

Peter spotted a small group of climbers on the Lhotse Face heading for the South Col. They were just tiny specks but still stood out clearly against the brilliant white of the snow and ice. They were so tiny that we had to watch them for quite some time before we could convince ourselves that they were actually on the move. As my eyes grew more accustomed to the task, I then spotted another party of climbers heading for the South Summit. It was staggering to think that whereas I was now standing higher than I had ever stood in my life, the summit of Everest, which was the goal of these climbers, was another 10,000 feet higher. I was now at about 18,500 feet but still had to crane my neck to see the top of Everest.

By this time most of our own group had reached the summit of Kala Pattar and were taking photographs or simply absorbing the views, mostly in silence. A few had walked as far as they had wished to go, looked at the scenery, taken photographs and turned downhill again. But those of us at the summit lingered there for perhaps half an hour, simply taking it all in. Eventually people started to drift back towards camp. Peter and I were the last to leave, with Lakpa.

Back at our camp I'm dog tired and feel as if I've been on a full day's hill walk. Peter is very tired too. In fact we both decide to climb back into our sleeping bags and sleep for a couple of hours. When I wake up I have an unpleasant headache, a sure sign that we've been higher during the day to a point where the air is even thinner. Luckily for me, the paracetamol takes the edge off the worst of it. I open the tent flap to step outside and discover that it's now snowing! The brilliant sunshine of just a couple of hours ago has been replaced by low cloud. I can't help thinking once again how fortunate we were with the weather this morning.

Late afternoon someone arrives from Base Camp with news of the main climbing expedition. It seems as though Team 2, which includes Brian Blessed, are on their way down. Team 1 is currently on the Lhotse Face. It isn't clear from the report whether that team is on its way up or down. There's no indication that anyone has reached the summit yet. The report seems to suggest that Brian Blessed had spent a night on his own on the South Col. This is the notch between Everest and Lhotse and stands at nearly 26,000 feet. From everything I've read, I can't imagine this could possibly be a pleasant experience for anyone, even if the weather were good which it rarely is there. The South Col is a vast and desolate area where expeditions set up an advanced camp before making an attempt on the summit. It is known to be a bitterly cold place where there can be tremendously high winds. It has also been called the highest dumping ground in the world and is strewn with abandoned tents and discarded equipment from many expeditions. There are frozen corpses there too. Hardly a cheering place to spend a night alone. The question on my mind is why Brian was on his own. My guess is that he probably wanted to make an attempt on the summit without supplementary oxygen and that the others - who were carrying oxygen - left him behind when he was no longer able to keep up with them.

Whatever it may be like on the South Col, down here our group is showing clear signs of the effects of our climb up Kala Pattar. Everyone is complaining of a headache. Vivienne is reminding us of the importance of drinking more and more water. She reminds us, correctly, that loss of appetite is one of the symptoms of altitude sickness but that our bodies still actually need nourishment. So this evening, in our communal tent, we make ourselves eat as much as we can face. No-one seems to be enjoying their food though. But the conversation is flowing and the general mood is positive. Everyone who climbed Kala Pattar, which is all of us except Elaine, is clearly very proud of the achievement and all the talk is of the stupendous views and the struggle to climb the hill. All Elaine can do is listen. Tactfully Phil keeps his words to a minimum but his broad smile tells us that he really enjoyed his day.

The other subject of conversation this evening is our trek tomorrow along the Khumbu Glacier to the famous Everest Base Camp. The talk is of one last big effort, one final push. I think people may have forgotten that the walk over the Cho La in a few days' time will involve far more height gain than tomorrow's trek but I stay silent on that subject. It's good to see that despite the fact that everyone is tired there's still plenty of enthusiasm for more walking.

It occurs to me that for some in our group the trek to Base Camp might actually be more important than today's climb. As for myself, I'm certainly looking forward to walking along the glacier, walking among the weird seracs and also to joining the members of the main climbing party, Brian Blessed among them possibly.

No-one lingers very long in the communal tent this evening. After dinner everyone drifts away to their tents for an early night. Except me. I decide I'm going to go across the moraine to the one tea house here in Gorak Shep. From our camp I can see lanterns burning inside the tea house and a change of scene appeals to me. I wonder who's over there. Even with my headtorch, crossing the moraine is tricky. The ground is stony and very uneven. However, I manage to negotiate the two hundred metre or so walk in about ten minutes.

I open the door of the tea house and of course everyone inside looks at me. I come face to face with the owner who welcomes me warmly as do the members of his family - his wife and two little children. At the far end of the main room I see what I suppose to be another trekking group. I go over to join them and they too greet me warmly, though I suspect they are tired. I find this hard to reconcile with the fact that they are all young - in their twenties, I would say, certainly younger than all the members of our group. They are from the Far East. Most do not speak English but their leader speaks it well. He asks me various questions about our group and I answer him. He is surprised to learn that we're intending to tackle the Cho La. He tells me that this had been his group's aim too but in his view they are no longer well enough to attempt it. When he tells me that they have taken no days off to rest and acclimatize, I can't help feeling sorry for them all. I stay for a cup of tea before heading off back to camp.

As I make my way back from the tea house in the dark, I'm still thinking about this group of youngsters who have been marched too fast through the thin air from Lukla and who are now clearly facing the consequences. I'm perhaps focusing rather too much on them and not enough on where I'm placing my feet as, suddenly, a stone gives way under my left foot and I feel my ankle twist sharply. It feels like a nasty sprain and I limp the final one hundred metres or so back into camp wondering whether - in a split second of carelessness - I've ruined my chances of getting to Base Camp tomorrow.

Back in our tent, Peter makes a quick assessment of my foot and says I shouldn't worry about it. Nothing is broken he declares confidently and as far as he can tell no ligaments have been torn. The fact that I was able to put weight on it is a good sign too, he says. However, if tomorrow morning I discover my foot has swollen overnight, I might have to stay put. These final words seem to undo the reassuring effects of his previous words but my overall impression is that he doesn't believe there will be a problem. I think he's just covering himself in case my foot does swell up unexpectedly.

We chat for a while as we clamber into our sleeping bags fully dressed and pull on our hats and gloves. In my excitement I reflect once again on the day's achievements and in particular the views from the summit of Kala Pattar. I notice Peter doesn't seem quite as talkative as I am, but I don't attach any particular significance to this. I curl up in my sleeping bag and I'm soon in the arms of Morpheus.

I hadn't been asleep long when I became aware that Peter was moving around. I turned and although it was very dark in the tent I could somehow tell that he was sitting up. He was fumbling for something.

'I'm not feeling that great,' were his first words to me. 'I need to find some tablets I've got somewhere here in my bag.'

'Use your head torch,' I said, realising he had been struggling in the dark rather than risk waking me up.

I asked Peter what the problem was and he said he was feeling some discomfort in his chest. By 'chest' I immediately understood 'heart' and felt slightly alarmed. I said nothing about this of course. Peter himself seemed calm but I sensed that inside he was uneasy. He took his own pulse and muttered something to himself.

Peter chose this moment to tell me that he had kept another secret from the trek organisers. He confided in me that he had a heart condition which had recurred from time to time over the years. As he hadn't been troubled by it for a while he had decided to keep the matter to himself rather than risk being refused a place on the expedition. I kept my silence on the question as to whether or not this had been a wise - or fair - thing to do. He now took two tablets and said - without a great deal of conviction, I felt - that he should be alright as these tablets had always worked well in the past. Quite what the tablets were I have no idea but he said something about thinning the blood and relaxing the muscles around the heart. He took some paracetamols as well.

Peter lay down and tried to sleep. I lay there listening. He tossed and turned for a while but then sat up again. He took his pulse once more and muttered to himself again. I was now starting to feel more than a little worried. Here we were, miles from anywhere and without any form of transport other than our yaks. In the dead of night things can always seem much worse than they actually are, of course, but I couldn't help feeling that I might at any moment have a medical emergency on my hands. And I certainly wasn't in a position to be able to help in an emergency. It was obvious to me that nothing could be done for Peter before daylight and even then I wasn't sure what arrangements could be made. The situation seemed to me all the worse somehow because I was with a qualified doctor who might ultimately prove to be unable to treat himself.

'I don't think they're working in the usual way,' he said, worryingly. 'The pain around my heart isn't getting any less. But at least it's getting no worse.'

Several difficult hours now followed during which Peter continued to monitor his heart rate every now and then. I was desperate to sleep but knew I needed to stay awake and keep him company, reassure him as best I could and talk to him about anything he wished and whatever subject came into my head. He sat up next to me most of the time with his fists clenched over his heart. From time to time he would lie down and I would take this as a sign that the pain was easing. But he was only doing it to change position and rest his arms. He said at one point that he didn't want to drop off to sleep in case something should happen to him. By this I wasn't sure whether he meant that he might suddenly wake up in agony or whether he was afraid he might not wake up at all.

Inwardly I was by now tearing my hair out but realised I had to continue to appear calm. All I could do was hope Peter could make it through the night so that we could make arrangements in the morning to evacuate him. Selfishly, I desperately wanted not to miss out on Base Camp if my foot were up to it and I was bitterly aware of the terrible irony of my position. Here I was sharing a tent with the only doctor on the expedition and I might end up having to accompany him down to lower ground. I kept trying to dismiss these selfish thoughts but it was difficult. I was torn. In the meantime I kept feeling that daylight simply couldn't come soon enough. There was no way I could lead Peter to lower ground in the dark. I could only hope that his condition didn't deteriorate.

But it did. The pain in Peter's chest became gradually worse as the night wore on. He knew that this was as a result of the altitude we were at. His blood simply wasn't getting enough oxygen and it was putting a strain on his heart. He was now taking his pulse more frequently. It was obvious to me that the results were making him increasingly anxious. He started to grow more and more agitated and I was becoming truly alarmed. As a qualified doctor he must have been fully aware of what was going on inside him and of the possible complications and consequences.

Peter was trying very hard to keep a lid on his emotions, not least because he probably realised that any additional stress would make things worse and that there was no help at hand. He kept saying that perhaps the drugs would work just well enough to get him through to the morning. But as time went by and the pain in his chest grew worse his words started to sound less convincing. I had done my best to try and be calm and reassure him in any way I could but inwardly I was now growing fearful for him and imagining the worst.

It was still pitch black outside and though dawn couldn't now be very far off, I felt an overwhelming urge to go for help before the situation got any worse. I can no longer remember the exact sequence of events but I think Peter and I came to the same conclusion at about the same time. Perhaps it was the effect of hearing me put it into words that made Peter finally accept that he needed outside help.

I picked up my headtorch and told Peter that I was going to wake Vivienne. Once the decision was made I wasted no time. I knew Vivienne left her hat outside her tent with her boots so that we could tell which tent was hers in case we should need her. I called her name quietly but got no response. I called a second time, a little louder, but still there came no response. The third time I simply called her name out loud and this worked. I heard her shuffling about inside and then her head appeared through the tent door. I quickly explained the situation. Without delay she tore herself from her sleeping bag, grabbed a medical kit - which I knew would be useless - and rushed with me back to our tent. By this time the seriousness of his condition was alarming even Peter and he was groaning loudly.

Vivienne spoke to Peter but could see straight away that she needed to take urgent action. He was now starting to find breathing very difficult. Vivienne disappeared into the night and returned in a few minutes with Lakpa and a porter. A bizarre scene now followed as the porter and Lakpa somehow got Peter into a wicker basket which the porter then picked up and slung over his shoulders. I watched in bewilderment as Peter disappeared into the night on the back of the porter, his legs dangling out from the bottom of the basket.

I went back to the tent, giddy from what I'd been through, and got into my sleeping bag still full of concern for poor Peter. I may have dropped off to sleep but can't really remember. In no time at all, as it seemed to me, the two Sherpa women were at the tent door with their teapots. Behind their heads I could see the daylight which for hours during that awful night simply couldn't come quickly enough. They didn't seem surprised to find me on my own and smiled in their usual way. To that extent, at least, all was normal. I found this reassuring after a night of tension and anxiety.

# Wednesday 6 October

At breakfast all the talk is of Peter, understandably. Questions are fired at me in concerned tones. I keep the details to a minimum and say nothing about Peter's history of heart problems. I catch Vivienne's eye as I'm telling my tale of sleepless hours. She reminds us that Peter is on his way down and that in her experience it is losing height which is the crucial factor in recovery. It's a shame, she says, that he will miss out on the trip to Base Camp but she is quite sure that he will already be feeling better. She tries now to get us to focus on the day ahead and on the particular challenges posed by having to walk on the Khumbu Glacier. She emphasises the need for us all to move together today and to follow Lakpa and the other Sherpas closely. The yaks, she explains, will not be travelling with us because of what she calls the 'difficulties' of the terrain. She means the dangers of the terrain. I suddenly remember Peter's first words about 'discomfort' in his 'chest' when he probably actually meant 'pain' in his 'heart'.

After a sleepless night of anxiety about Peter, the effects of altitude, my poor appetite and all the rest of it, I feel I have little energy and find the trek to Base Camp very hard indeed. I can see I'm not the only one who is suffering though. We're all finding it hard going today following the steep climb up Kala Pattar yesterday, which has definitely sapped our strength.

Today's walk is very different to yesterday's. On the one hand it isn't as steep and we shan't be climbing as high. On the other hand the terrain itself is very difficult. Initially we're walking on the loose rock and stones of the moraine with patches of ice here and there and some flowing water just below the surface.

The ground is very uneven too and we seem to be forever going up and down unlike yesterday which was basically one long climb followed by a long descent. I'm relieved to find that my ankle is feeling better though.

Once we step onto the glacier itself conditions underfoot change again. There's enough of a covering of either stones or snow for us not to need crampons but we find ourselves meandering left and right to avoid various obstacles. Crevasses are the biggest threat early on in the day and we do long detours at times to avoid the most dangerous of these, sticking close to Lakpa and the other Sherpas throughout. In places where one side of a crevasse has collapsed we see huge walls of ice, perhaps sixty feet high. These walls are an indication of what lies under our feet as we make our way towards Base Camp.

The sky today is amazingly blue and the sun is beating down on us relentlessly. The sunlight also reflects off the ice and snow all around and we're all feeling hot. However, we have to protect every inch of our skin from the sun's rays and can't risk exposing any part of our bodies for any length of time. As we get higher, it seems that the whole world - apart from the sky - is white and the light is intensely bright, even with our sunglasses on. We're now in a wonderland of snow and ice, and when we reach the weird towers of the seracs it's as if we've suddenly stepped into some strange film set or a bizarre dream. These enormous columns or blocks of glacial ice, as high as houses, remind me of icebergs and look as if no force on earth could move them. But they can collapse suddenly and they present a constant danger. We have no choice but to weave our way between these eerie pinnacles which look so beautiful that you want to linger and observe them. But I notice Lakpa isn't lingering. He marches us through this dangerous area and only stops for us to rest once we're well away from the last of the seracs.

Despite the effect of the heat and of walking day after day at high altitude, I'm still overwhelmed by the sheer beauty and grandeur of the scenery. Everything here is on such an enormous scale too. The mountains are, obviously, much higher than any in Europe and the glaciers and other features are correspondingly bigger.

Add to these things the distances involved, the manpower needed to get our group here and the remoteness of the area and you start to get an idea of what an adventure this has been for us.

By mid-afternoon we are at Everest Base Camp. It feels amazing to be here, a place where there is so much mountaineering history. We have a late lunch outside our tents at the very foot of the famous Khumbu Icefall. There is nothing quite like the Icefall. It's an enormous jumble and crush of fractured ice tumbling steeply from the Western Cwm. The steepness of the slope beneath it creates enormous pressure on the glacial ice and it has huge cracks or crevasses, some hundreds of feet deep. The glacier itself is of course always on the move and new crevasses can open up without warning. They provide a constant threat to climbers. At the beginning of every walking season a new way has to be found through this confusion. Ropes are fixed at certain points to make it safer and easier to proceed. The safety is only relative though as new crevasses can appear at any time, swallowing people and equipment, and huge blocks of ice which seem unmovable can without warning simply collapse.

Base Camp is located at the outer edge of a sharp bend in the glacier. It covers a very large area at the top end of the valley, tucked under the slopes of the border mountains. We're not alone here. In fact, for almost as far as the eye can see at ground level, there are myriad tents belonging to climbing expeditions from different nationalities. In this city of tents there are currently expeditions from Japan, France, America and elsewhere, each country seemingly with its own colour tents. All this human activity is due to one thing alone - the presence of Everest. Not that you can actually see much of Everest from here, only the lower end of one of its ridges. The view at Base Camp is completely dominated by the Khumbu Icefall.

After lunch, which involves plenty of tea, we are on our way once more. This time we're only going as far as our main expedition tent, a short distance away. In this huge tent, which is headquarters for the climbers and their support team, we are greeted by Tim who is in charge of the radio and Simon who seems to be in charge of stores.

Simon offers us Jaffa Cakes, the first chocolate I've tasted for a fortnight. Delicious. I ask him if I can have another and he holds out the box to me.

We are soon told by Tim in answer to my question that Brian Blessed is now down in the Western Cwm and in camp there. He will be returning to Base Camp tomorrow but isn't expected until late afternoon. I feel disappointed to be missing him. We will be back at Gorak Shep - if not at Lobuche - by tomorrow afternoon according to our revised itinerary and will effectively be one day ahead of him. But there is good news about Team 1. They will be going for the summit tomorrow and conditions are currently ideal. The forecast is good too.

The rest of the afternoon and early evening disappear and before we know it the light begins to fade once more. As soon as the sun drops out of sight the temperature plummets dramatically. We may have been overheating earlier today on the glacier but now I'm wearing several layers as well as my hat and gloves. I can feel my feet getting cold when I stand still for any length of time. Even in our communal tent, where we meet for our evening meal, we're all wearing more layers than usual and nearly everyone is wearing a hat too. Some are actually shivering.

It comes as no surprise that one of Vivienne's themes for her evening briefing is the cold here at Base Camp. Unnecessarily, I feel, she suggests we wear several layers of clothing in bed. As our heads will be poking out of our sleeping bags, she says we should wear a hat as well. She tells us that we can all fill metal drinking bottles with hot water from the main expedition tent for use as a hot water bottle but also warns us not to bring them into direct contact with our skin. She adds that she's not telling us this because of the danger of burning or scalding ourselves but because, by morning, the water may have frozen and we may find the bottle frozen to our skin.

Vivienne then tells us not to be shy about sleeping very close to whoever we're sharing a tent with. It's important, she says, to huddle together for extra warmth. There is some mirth as she speaks but I'm aware that now that Peter has gone I have a tent to myself. At this point she says that no-one should be on their own in a tent and I feel a shudder run through me as I remember that the only other person currently on his own is Richard. I'm relieved to hear her then say that Richard is to rejoin his original partner, Jason, for tonight and that I will be sharing with Jonathan who began the expedition with a tent to himself but agreed at one point to let Jason join him, thus leaving Richard on his own.

As we leave the communal tent to retire for the evening, I'm struck by the amazing view overhead. I can see thousands of stars and the Milky Way is perfectly clear. I remember the stunning night sky at Tengboche but feel sure that this view is even better. The sheer number of stars is overwhelming. They appear to completely fill the sky and give the impression that there's more light than darkness up there - that the stars occupy more room that the space between them.

We make our way back very gingerly to our tents. The terrain underfoot is treacherous. The whole area is an ice rink covered with an uneven layer of debris. You're forever changing direction to avoid piles of stones or the occasional break in the ice. One moment you're being careful not to turn your ankle on a rock, the next you're stepping over or going around a patch of exposed ice. There are also tiny streams and small pools of water here and there. We all exercise great care as no-one wants to risk injury in such an inhospitable place as this. However, one of our number, the charming Mark, put his weight on some ice which cracked immediately and he found himself up to his knee in freezing water. Why do these things always happen to the nice people?

Our tent is pitched on the thick ice of the glacier. The Sherpas have laid an additional loose, rubber groundsheet - sometimes called a footprint groundsheet - on top of the ice to increase insulation. It's still cold inside the tent though. Jonathan and I both start the night wearing all our clothes. I'm wearing two pairs of walking socks, a pair of thermal trousers underneath my walking trousers, a thermal top, a shirt and two fleeces as well as my walking jacket, though this eventually comes off as it makes too much noise every time I turn in my sleeping bag. I have a hot water bottle which I place on my tummy between my two fleeces to keep my core warm. I have two extra companions with me in my sleeping bag this evening. These are my boots. They are slightly wet following a day walking on ice and snow and I don't want them to freeze overnight.

I wake up during the night. Though I'm comfortably warm in my sleeping bag, the air around me is bitterly cold. I simply can't imagine what it must be like outside our tent. Could anyone actually survive a night outdoors here? It feels to me as if we're relying on the very material of the tent to keep us alive, to act as a thin and flimsy barrier between ourselves and death. My definition of cold changes during this night at Base Camp. The cold here is still, silent and threatening. It challenges you.

It warns you that if you make a single mistake it will pounce on you and punish you for it. One thing's for sure, I'm very glad I bought that extra bottle in Namche!

As I lay awake, I can't help thinking about the well-nigh insufferable heat Jane and I had to face when trying to sleep at some friends' house in Bordeaux one summer some years ago. It was thirty six degrees Celsius in our bedroom one evening. Because of the nuisance of mosquitos we weren't able to open our windows. Even as it was we slept under mosquito nets. I remember we doused our sheets with cold water several times during that night in an attempt to cool down.

I remember something else too as I lay awake. This was something Vivienne had uttered during dinner in a way that suggested it wasn't of any particular importance. She casually mentioned that we only have one day's supply of food left and that we need to get back to Gorak Shep tomorrow to restock. I can't help wondering what would happen if the weather were to deteriorate suddenly and the visibility were too poor for us to get out of Base Camp. Could the Sherpas find their way along the glacier in such conditions? With these cheering thoughts I draw my knees up to my chest once more and make myself as small as I can.

# Thursday 7 October

In the morning, Jonathan tells me cheerfully that it's minus fifteen degrees inside our tent. The extra layers have done the job, however, and inside my sleeping bag I'm really quite cosy. My hot water bottle hasn't actually frozen but the water is certainly too cold to drink. My boots haven't frozen either, I'm delighted to note. Jonathan tells me in his nonchalant way that he has left his boots outside the tent - as he always does, he says - because they smell. We laugh when we discover that they will now also need to be thawed out.

We have our breakfast in the main expedition tent this morning. This puts everyone in a good mood. The atmosphere here is bright and cheerful. There is a great deal of anticipation in the air too as the climbing team high up on the mountain is going to make a summit bid today. If the conditions remain good, as they have been so far, the expedition could place a record number of climbers on the summit of Everest in one day, including Ramon Blanco Suarez who at 60 years of age would be the oldest Everest summiteer in history.

Everyone is interested in Brian Blessed's progress as he is the best known member of the climbing team. At one point we hear he is still in the Western Cwm and feeling tired. We learn more about his time on the South Col where, it's now confirmed, he had indeed been on his own. The news reported to us is that he did set off alone in the direction of the summit. It seems that he insisted on making his attempt without oxygen and so he wasn't able to keep pace with the rest of the team who had the double advantage of being more experienced than him and also that they were carrying oxygen bottles and were therefore able to make better progress.

We meet some of the climbers who have been into the Western Cwm. It's exciting to hear first-hand accounts of the wonderful world above the Icefall - the world we won't be seeing as we don't have permission to go any further than Base Camp. They tell us of the difficulties and the dangers they faced, particularly whilst moving up and down through the Icefall, which some of them have done several times. I ask about snow conditions in the Western Cwm where avalanches are a constant threat, the climb up and down the steep and icy Lhotse Face and about life in camp on the South Col. I've read so much about these places over the years and I enjoy this rare opportunity to rub shoulders with mountaineers of their calibre and gain an insight into their world.

We're not able to use any of the main expedition supplies but I do help myself to another Jaffa Cake when I see the box lying around. Simon must have spotted my slightly guilty look as I eyed up the box once again later. 'Help yourself,' he said with a broad smile. 'We've got more than we can possibly get through.' So I take two. I put one in my mouth and the other I put in my pocket - wrapped in a serviette - for later. In the meantime I can see that Tim the radio man is showing Vivienne how she can stay in touch with Base Camp for the next day or so using a small handset he gives her. This way we'll be able to get all the latest news on the climbers and their summit attempts.

It was another glorious day. We made our way back along the Khumbu Glacier to Gorak Shep where we had lunch. I was quite tired by this time. It had been a very warm morning and the sun had been reflected mercilessly off the ice and the snow on the mountains all around us. Even the slightest uphill pull was exhausting. The scenery, of course, was as stunning as ever. As we passed the giant seracs on the glacier, I had to remind myself occasionally to take it all in and not focus so much on how tired I was feeling. After all, I wasn't likely to be returning here ever.

During the afternoon we continued south to Lobuche. Gradually it clouded over. After the excitement of climbing Kala Pattar, the thrill of being in Base Camp and of meeting some of the climbing team, it's an anti-climax to be trudging along the moraine once again. We're all delighted when Vivienne announces that we are to have a rest day tomorrow. This is excellent news as everyone is weary.

With our late afternoon tea we get more good news. A letter arrives by runner. It is from Peter. It seems his porter carried him all the way to Pheriche where he started to improve immediately, there being more oxygen in the air for him to breathe. In the letter, Vivienne tells us, he says he is feeling much better and is looking forward to rejoining us. Vivienne reads only snippets and says she will read the whole letter to us this evening at dinner. I'm missing Peter's company and am looking forward to seeing him again soon. I feel sorry that he missed out on our visit to Base Camp but remind myself that he did at least climb Kala Pattar, something he will always remember.

I think I realise now why he kept quiet at first about being a doctor. He must have been fully aware that for anyone to travel to the Himalaya with a heart condition like his would be seen by many as foolish, not to say reckless. How much worse for a doctor to do it. He certainly took a risk. I choose not to dwell on the possibility that things could have turned out much worse for him or on the impact this would have had on the rest of us. Likewise I choose not to ask myself whether it was right for him to conceal his condition from the organisers who might have decided he shouldn't be allowed to come on the expedition in the first place.

Vivienne has more news for us. A further report from Base Camp tells us that Brian had made it back safely through the Khumbu Icefall and was at that very moment approaching Base Camp. An unconfirmed report suggests that he had witnessed a terrifying avalanche whilst at the South Col and that this had made him reconsider proceeding any further on his own. But the best mountaineering news comes a few minutes later when Simon at Base Camp calls us again to announce that all the members of Team 1 have made it to the summit. There are loud cheers.

# Friday 8 October

At breakfast this morning Elaine declared firmly that there was 'absolutely no way' that she would be attempting to cross the Cho La. She had been sitting quietly next to Phil up to this point but in an astonishing and unexpected outburst - memorable for its vehemence - she suddenly released an impressive verbal assault. First, she spewed out a long list of complaints about the trek and its lack of organisation, as she saw it. She followed this with a diatribe against Vivienne in particular, but she also singled out one or two members of our group who had dared on previous occasions to defend Vivienne in an attempt to get Elaine to see things from a guide's point of view. Next came a sequence of unflattering observations about the rest of us as a unit which, of course, only served to isolate Elaine completely. In an eruption of anger which was growing increasingly embarrassing she threw in some remarkable gems - 'Switzerland is better than Nepal because you can get good meals in the hotels in the mountains' and 'mountains are all the same everywhere' and 'I'd rather be in Spain'. When the torrent of words finally came to an end, she stormed off to her tent. Phil followed meekly.

Needless to say, these remarks were the occasion for great mirth afterwards as the rest of us stood outside the communal tent on an amazingly beautiful morning surrounded by some of the most stunning scenery on the planet. Talking in near whispers, someone wondered what the mountain scenery might be like in Torremolinos. Someone else asked whether a hotel couldn't be built for tourists at Base Camp or perhaps a café on the summit of Everest itself, like the one on Snowdon. Sand, buckets, spades and ice cream were all mentioned too. Some sympathy was expressed for Phil who had listened to Elaine's outburst with a look of complete resignation, as if he had heard it all before or perhaps knowing that there was nothing he could do to stem the flow once it had begun.

It's a curious thing about us humans that though we had just witnessed a soul in torment who obviously needed our support and encouragement, she had so managed to alienate everyone with a few rather too candid and badly-chosen words that as a result no-one seemed to feel any sympathy for her whatsoever. Probably the opposite. She appeared to have united everyone against her. Vivienne now approached us - doubtless feeling very hurt but also realising that she must act - and said that she would give Elaine time to cool down and visit her in her tent later. She said she was convening a meeting for the rest of us back inside the communal tent so that we could have a frank and open discussion on health and other issues.

Stuart begins by reporting that he was unwell last night and did not sleep at all. He has been sick today but now feels better, he says. Jason had a bad night at Base Camp and had to wake Vivienne at some point. He says he feels alright today though. And so it goes on. We all tell our tales of woe. Everyone has suffered in one way or another. And it is nothing to do with fitness. Stuart, for example, is a marathon runner but he has had the usual headaches, loss of appetite and difficulty sleeping at times. His wife, Cath, is the only person among us who doesn't appear to have suffered much, though she too has had her problems. She tries to lighten the mood of the discussion by saying that she had grazed her knee on a rock earlier today. There is a little laughter. What's striking though is that most of us report similar symptoms. More than one person expresses my own view that with more time to acclimatize we would all have enjoyed our adventure a good deal more but that we regard the symptoms we've suffered as a price worth paying.

There's a more relaxed atmosphere now that views and concerns have been given an airing. As it's warm and as we have plenty of time on our hands, we take the opportunity to have a thoroughly good wash and also to wash some of our clothes and hang them out to dry in the glorious sunshine. These jobs done, people sit around reading, talking, playing cards and generally taking it easy.

During the afternoon we play an improvised version of boules using stones of a suitable size. The Sherpas and porters look at us in amusement as we laugh and squeal at various points. Next we play French cricket using someone's walking pole for a bat and some rolled up socks for a ball. The Sherpas and porters look at us in even greater amusement as they try to work out the rules of this odd game. Running up and down is still surprisingly tiring so we soon revert to the much gentler pastime of boules. The object of this game is easier for Sherpas and porters to work out and soon we invite them to join us. I notice that it's only the men who can be enticed to play. But in any case we all have a really good laugh together and in its own way this was one of the most enjoyable episodes in our whole journey.

I've had such fun that I decide I may even allow myself a beer this evening. This would involve a visit to one of the tea houses which might also perhaps provide the opportunity to meet some new people. Then, as I walk around our camp, I spot someone using a mirror outside their tent. I ask if I can borrow it for a moment. I remember that I haven't seen my face for almost two weeks. When I look in the mirror I decide I may even treat myself to a shave - perhaps before I go for that beer.

During dinner, Vivienne reminds us that there's still a good deal of climbing to do before we finally lose height and start making our way slowly back to Lukla. Tomorrow we will turn along a different valley and leave the immediate environs of Everest. We will head up this valley and camp some way below the Cho La. The following day we will climb over the Cho La and from that point onwards our journey will be for the most part downhill.

Vivienne now reads Peter's letter to us in full. I had assumed that he would be meeting us just above Pheriche and that he would be coming with us along the new side valley and over the Cho La pass. But it seems he is to take a lower route as it would be too risky for him to start gaining height again. The Cho La therefore is out of the question. We will next see him in a village called Phortse, on our way back to Namche Bazaar. I feel dismayed that I shan't see him again for several days. As I'm pondering this, Vivienne then tells us that Elaine and Phil will not be accompanying us over the Cho La either. There is silence as she announces this. Everyone sits stock still, including Elaine and Phil. Phil is looking a little sheepish but Elaine wears a determined look. Vivienne doesn't elaborate and simply moves on.

Towards the end of the evening I suddenly start to feel light-headed for some unknown reason. I also find that I'm struggling to focus my eyes on things in front of me. Understandably I find this more than a little alarming. It's also unexpected. I thought any symptoms of altitude sickness would subside as we lost height but now I'm facing something new. Vivienne looks in her medical book but can't find any illness to which my symptoms belong. I decide on an early night - beer now being the very last thing I want - and I go off to my tent feeling really worried. As the light-headedness and my inability to focus grow worse, I find myself staggering rather than walking back to the tent. Eventually I'm able to crawl into my sleeping bag and lie on my back. My head continues to spin but in the dark I can no longer tell whether my eyes are still unable to focus.

This is actually the lowest point in the whole trip for me as I lie in my bed worrying about what's wrong with me and wondering whether I will ever see home again.

# Saturday 9 October

In the morning, when I wake up, it's a huge relief to discover that my head is fine and that I'm seeing straight once again. I remember that I had been sitting quite close to one of the kerosene lamps at dinner, that I was vaguely aware at the time of the unpleasant fumes but that I had chosen to ignore this. I now conclude that it must have been the fumes that caused those awful and worrying symptoms last night. But rather like Scrooge, when he wakes up following the visits from the three Christmas ghosts, I'm so happy to be alive and well that my focus is now firmly on the day ahead and not on what happened last night.

We're late setting off on our day's walk. The delay is largely due to Elaine and Phil as a matter of fact. Vivienne tries to talk them out of their decision to go down. I think she deliberately delayed their departure by a day in the hope that a rest day would help Elaine to see things in a different light. But this morning she was equally adamant that she did not want to go over the Cho La with the rest of us. None of us really knows what Phil would actually like to do, given the choice. In the meantime their belongings have been loaded onto the most heavily-laden porter I've seen on the entire expedition. He is carrying on his back virtually all the belongings of both Phil and Elaine as well as his own. I'm in awe and am simply staggered that anyone could possibly lift such a weight off the ground, let alone carry it for several miles.

We all say goodbye to Phil and Elaine and we are all polite despite the harsh words we had heard. We watch them set off and as soon as they're out of earshot the jokes and sarcastic comments begin once more. Phil and Elaine, without knowing it, keep us entertained all day.

In the meantime, we headed downhill from Lobuche and just before we reached the Sherpa memorials we turned right into a new valley. We were now walking in the direction of the Cho La, a high snow-covered pass which will present the last major views of our tour. From there we will see the enormous bulk of Cho Oyu. Then we will descend into yet another new valley and head gently back to Namche.

It wasn't a long walk for us today and though we have had to regain a lot of height we were not as tired perhaps as we'd expected when we arrived in camp. No sooner had we reached camp than the cloud came down. As ever, Madhu and her cheerful companion appeared immediately with our tea. And as ever it was very welcome, particularly as the temperature began to plummet suddenly once the cloud engulfed us and our camp to such an extent that we couldn't even see many of the tents. After that first cuppa, we made our way into the communal tent for yet more tea or coffee.

Inside the tent, everyone was in a talkative mood. I attributed this largely to the fact that our trek for the day was over but also to the fact that Elaine was no longer with us. She was the butt of many jokes throughout our walk today and it was obvious that her thoughtless - not to say abusive - comments about the rest of us had served to draw us closer together. It struck me once more that there's nothing quite like having a common enemy for uniting people.

Late afternoon we started drifting off to our tents. I decided to have a nap. In no time at all, as it seemed to me, we were being summoned back to the communal tent for our evening meal. Once again, I noticed straight away that there was an altogether more relaxed atmosphere in the tent than we'd been used to recently and that everyone was on good form. We ate a hearty meal which we all enjoyed. For the first time on our journey we actually had spaghetti. I wondered whether this had somehow been pilfered from the main expedition tent at Base Camp and whether Simon was missing it.

Vivienne reminded us that there was now only a little over a week before we would be back in our own beds. Everyone cheered at the very thought. And therefore, Vivienne proceeded, it was all the more important that we make the best of our final few days in the Himalaya. I for one agreed wholeheartedly with this. I was looking forward very much to crossing the Cho La and taking a different return route to Namche.

After we had eaten, the tables were cleared and we started playing cards. Someone produced a box of fruit pastilles from somewhere. We had all been told to bring with us on our trek a secret stash of our favourite sweets or chocolate. The appearance of the fruit pastilles seemed like yet another sign that there was now greater unity and more camaraderie in camp.

# Sunday 10 October

I slept well last night and this morning felt ready to face the hard, steep climb up to the Cho La. But the climb proved much harder than I had anticipated and I found myself panting for breath as we gained height and having to pause every few steps. It was the same for all of us and progress was very slow.

But even had I been ready for the climb, I certainly wasn't ready for the conditions we discovered as we approached the top of the pass. We reached the snowline late morning and before long it started to strike me that the snow - which was at first soft and gave way easily under the weight of our boots - was getting much harder. As there was still quite a way to go to the top of the pass and a lot of height to gain, I couldn't help wondering what the conditions would be like up there. Not far below the high point, I found myself having to kick the edges of my boots into the hard snow and wishing I had crampons and an ice axe for protection. I was amazed to see, though, that the porters were now walking bare-footed, carrying their usual heavy loads, and were making much better progress than us.

In the meantime our group was slowing down and people were starting to lose their balance and the odd tumble was taken. I could see that Vivienne was concerned. She had every reason to be. The conditions were no longer safe for us. When we reached the top of the pass, she urged us to be cautious as we advanced down the slope on the opposite side. She told us that it had been unusually cold and that she hadn't expected the snow to be frozen, as it now was. I could tell that Lakpa too was concerned. I wasn't privy to the discussion he and Vivienne had at this point but wished I could be. In fact I felt we should all have been asked our view. Whatever factors were considered, the decision taken was that we should continue. I wasn't at all sure as most accidents happen in descent.

Things now started to go wrong and it is only by luck that there were no serious injuries during the first part of our way down into the valley ahead. There was only a short steep section to negotiate - perhaps no more than two hundred feet - before we would reach safer ground, free of snow. Almost immediately, however, someone lost their footing and started to slide away. With no ice axes available there was no way of self-arresting. If you want to self-arrest on hard snow or ice, it has to be done straight away. Otherwise the rate of acceleration downhill on a surface with no friction makes stopping yourself virtually impossible. You become a mere helpless object. I watched as the person who fell accelerated past boulders in the snow, missing them by inches, and came to a stop as her jacket somehow wrapped itself around a smaller boulder lower down. It was only when she stood up that I could see it was Gwen. Hers was a very lucky escape.

Before Gwen was able to rejoin us, Richard lost his footing. He was more fortunate though and almost immediately managed to grab a boulder sticking up through the surface of the snow. It was my turn next. Sure enough, I was soon on my side and sliding downhill fast. Realising I had no means of stopping myself, I relaxed and went with it, looking ahead to see if there might be anything lower down which I could seize to slow myself down or stop myself going any further. There was nothing. Besides I was soon travelling too fast to be able to grab hold of anything. It was now a matter of avoiding the rocks. Entirely by luck, I narrowly missed a large boulder by a couple of inches. Had I struck it at that speed I would undoubtedly have sustained a serious injury. I somehow managed to roll onto my back and keep my feet pointing downhill. Ahead of me there then appeared a smaller rock. I was heading straight towards it and instinctively braced myself for a collision. It was again more by luck than anything else that I managed to get both feet against the rock which brought me to a juddering halt.

Poor Mark was not so fortunate. He too lost his footing on the hard snow just below the top of the pass and I saw him slide straight towards a rock which jutted slightly above the surface of the snow. He bounced upwards off this and continued to accelerate downhill, unable to do anything to help himself. He then struck a larger boulder lower down on the slope. He took a glancing blow which stopped him for just long enough for him to be able to make a grab for the rock and bring himself to a halt.

The three of us who had taken long falls - Gwen, Mark and I - made our way slowly across the face of the slope, moving from rock to rock, until eventually we reached softer snow. In the meantime Pauline also slipped, lower down on the descent from the col, but fortunately she soon came to rest in the softer snow. However she was badly shaken, both by the other falls she had witnessed and by her own fall, and had to be carried some distance afterwards by Lakpa on his back. Patricia too had to be helped almost all the way down from the Cho La. Others were holding onto each other and groping their way slowly downhill.

There were several more stumbles but no more serious falls. Vivienne was deeply concerned and was doubtless aware that things could have ended far worse than they did. I was shaken by my fall but so relieved to have missed that large boulder and to have survived unscathed that I was reduced to silence. Poor Mark was bleeding from his nose and from a cut just above his right eye. His wounds needed immediate attention which he received from Vivienne. I was thinking about Peter and how good it would be to have him with us at this point.

I think I was more embarrassed than anything by my fall. A silly reaction really as there was nothing I could have done to prevent it. To all enquiries I quietly insisted I was alright. Someone then told me that there was a tear in my jacket. When I inspected it I found that I had also torn through my other layers and that my elbow was exposed to the air. I had a graze on it and decided I had better have it cleaned up and dressed.

We were soon below the hard snow and walking on softer snow which supported us well. Within a quarter of an hour or so we were out of the snow altogether and the walking became easy. At one point, where there was an area of flat ground, Vivienne called us all together. Still shaken and concerned, she said something which I took at the time to be an effort to deflect any responsibility for what had happened from herself. Perhaps she was worried that there would be complaints and perhaps she was concerned about her reputation and future prospects. But it wasn't her best moment of the tour. I wasn't inwardly blaming her or anyone else for my tumble anyway, as a matter of fact. I blamed the snow and the fact that I had no crampons. It was clear though that the decision to cross this high pass, once the conditions underfoot were known, had been a mistake which could have caused serious injuries or could even - heaven forbid - have cost lives.

I think fatigue contributed to these falls too. It was a big pull up to the Cho La on a warm morning at high altitude. There were signs that I had acclimatized well but by the time I reached the top of the Cho La I was more tired than I can ever recall after any walk. Given the accumulated tiredness we all felt from walking over the course of many days at altitude, it was perhaps not the best of decisions to press on.

Whatever the rights and the wrongs of it, we had made it over the Cho La and could now regroup in the knowledge that most of the walking from here on would be downhill and that there were no more serious obstacles to overcome. The mood among the group though was at a low point. We were all worn out by the climb and unsettled by our ordeal on the snow. We were also concerned for poor Mark. Vivienne now abandoned the original plan to push on to Na and camp was pitched for the night at our lunch spot, still high in the valley. Or perhaps it was Lakpa's decision.

Wounds were dressed, tea was taken and everyone rested in the late afternoon sunshine. Vivienne came around to ask how we all were. Mark was trying to remain cheerful but he was clearly in some discomfort. I'd never seen him reluctant to speak when spoken to but his answers were now monosyllabic. I knew he was feeling much worse than he admitted.

Vivienne approached me at one point and wondered whether I had any stories I could tell when we all gathered in the communal tent for our evening meal. I didn't really feel like telling stories but asked what she had in mind. She asked whether I had any tales about my walks in the mountains of Scotland but as the ones which sprang to mind involved an avalanche or poor decision-making I didn't think I should mention them to her. 'I know,' she said suddenly. 'You can tell us how you met Brian Blessed.' Then, seeming happy with her decision, off she went to ask the others if they too had stories. She had obviously decided that this would be a good way to lift spirits this evening.

I first met Brian Blessed after a talk he gave at our local theatre. When I was a boy he was the central character in an early BBC police drama called 'Z Cars'. I'd taken an interest in him ever since and had watched him in many and diverse roles. It was only later on in his career, of course, that he developed into the character we know today with the great booming voice. Loud and imposing he certainly can be, though.

Brian is a tall man. He is also well-built and terrifically strong, determined and tenacious. He stands out in any company. He looks - or glares - at you in a fixed, almost intimidating, way. But at the same time he is kind, well-meaning and, above all, positive in his outlook and in his approach to life. The impression he gave in his talk at the theatre that evening was of a very driven individual who had grown up in a working class area where prospects might, on the face of it, have seemed limited. But he had been brought up to believe in himself and his abilities, and had been encouraged to pursue his dreams. A recurring phrase of his that evening was 'Don't let the bastards grind you down!' In fact, these were his parting words as the curtain fell.

Brian's central message was that you should never be afraid to try and achieve your goals in life no matter how unrealistic they may appear to others. Another aspect of this message was that you should not pay heed to people (i.e. bastards!) who pour cold water on your plans. There are always people in the world who see the negative aspects of any situation first. The trick is to learn to ignore them and surround yourself with more encouraging individuals who sympathise with your aims and will give you at least verbal encouragement if not actual practical support.

My particular reason for wanting to see Brian at the theatre that evening was that he had recently written a book about his first attempt on Everest, on the northern side of the mountain, in Tibet. It was the fulfilling of a lifelong ambition for him to follow in the footsteps of his boyhood hero George Mallory who, in 1924, with Andrew Irvine, mysteriously disappeared near the summit of Everest. To this day no-one knows whether or not the two - or perhaps just one of them - actually reached the summit. Brian had read extensively on the early expeditions to Everest and was now keen to follow Mallory's route and also to wear the kind of clothing Mallory would have been wearing, rather than modern clothing. He also wanted to achieve this without supplementary oxygen. Brian's book was published to coincide with the release of a film about his adventure. The book, like the film, is really about people and their dreams. Everest, in this sense, is a symbol. Many - if not all - of us have ambitions which may seem unachievable. Both the book and the film can be seen as sources of encouragement and inspiration to others.

After his talk, Brian was signing copies of his book in the foyer. I queued up with everyone else and when my turn came I mentioned my own interest in Everest and mountaineering. He asked whether I was considering a visit to Nepal in the near future and when I told him that indeed I was he said he had a suggestion to make. Afterwards, in the bar, he told me that he had received an offer to accompany an international expedition on the south side of Everest, the Nepal side.

There was to be a support trek as far as Base Camp with the stated aim of helping in an environmental clean up. He asked whether I might be interested in joining the trek and gave me the organisers' details.

This, in essence, was the story I told my companions in the communal tent that evening. Vivienne, I discovered, had asked everyone else to tell a story that lasted about five to ten minutes. In this way, an hour and a half quickly went by and we heard all sorts of tales about school life, university life, life in the financial world, life in London and life in a sleepy Yorkshire village. It was not only an excellent way of cheering us all up - once we'd got going - but we also got to know a little more about each other. Maybe we should have done this on our first evening together in Kathmandu.

# Monday 11 October

Overall we have lost quite a bit of height on our walk today although it has been undulating at times with a good deal of up and down. After first crossing some uneven and then rocky ground, we followed an easy spur covered in short grass which gave pleasant walking. The head of the valley, behind us, was dominated by Cho Oyu and as we descended we followed the Ngozumpa glacier, way over to our right, which is the longest glacier in the Himalaya. The valley is home also to Gokyo Lakes which attract thousands of tourists every year. The Lakes are considered sacred by both Buddhists and Hindus. They stand at between 4,700 and 5,000 metres above sea level and are the world's highest freshwater lake system comprising six main lakes. Nearby, on the western side of the Ngozumpa glacier, is Gokyo Ri, a popular trekking peak which stands at just over 17,500 feet above sea level. So, although the valley feels and looks quite different to the area immediately around Everest, it has many attractions of its own and is really splendid.

As morning wore on, we descended into a greener, more hospitable and more fertile area. There was no doubt that we were now moving more quickly. Breathing was becoming easier too. As the route ahead was obvious, we had become spread out in little groups, each advancing at their own pace. There was a bit of a nasty surprise just before we arrived at our lunch spot though. A long and fairly steep pull got our hearts beating fast once more and the whole party slowed down to the kind of pace we'd been used to on the final days of our approach to the foot of Everest. It was a sharp reminder.

As we struggled up the final section into the hamlet of Thare, we had a surprise of a very different kind awaiting us. There, marching towards us with a great big smile on his face, was Peter. I hadn't expected to see him until we reached Phortse, much lower down, later in the day. It was like being reunited with a long lost friend, even though it had only been a few days since we'd seen each other.

The sun is shining and we eat our lunch outdoors, sitting in small groups. I'm quietly delighted when Peter comes automatically to sit with me. He has finished answering people's questions about his health and as he takes his lunch he starts to tell me in more detail about his trip down to Pheriche on the back of the porter. Understandably it had been a bumpy ride but Peter was too relieved to be losing height and moving towards possible help at Pheriche to worry about this. The porter had stayed with him at Pheriche for a day before accompanying him - with Peter now walking again - for a further two days back in the direction of Tengboche and then turning uphill into the valley where we now find ourselves. I gather Peter's porter is rather too fond of his raksi and chang which makes him extremely merry, prone to singing and farting and liable to fall over. It's good to hear Peter talking cheerfully again and we spend much of the rest of the day together.

It occurred to me as I was making my way slowly with Peter to the tea house for our evening meal, weaving our way in and out of the narrow terraces where the local people grow their crops, that our adventure was now almost at an end. The high ground was well behind us already and there would be no more discomfort caused by being at altitude. No more dreadfully cold nights either. Phortse, even though it's only home to a small community really, seems a metropolis compared to the remote and quite desolate places we've been in for the last week or so.

We enter the tea house which has been Peter's place of residence for two nights. Inside it's dark, dingy and smoky but there is a warm welcome from the owner and his family, and the atmosphere throughout the evening is homely and relaxed. We reflect on our day and most feel that it has been interesting and refreshing to see a new valley. Everyone also remarks on how good it is to be able to breathe normally again. After dinner the cards are brought out and when our jovial host asks whether any of us would like a beer, we all agree that this is a splendid idea. What an excellent day it has been!

# Tuesday 12 October

Today we dropped to the end of the valley and turned once more towards Namche Bazaar. We have now rejoined our outward route and there's a feeling of having come full circle. As I walk along with Peter at my side, I find the adventures we have lived through playing themselves like a film in my mind.

During the morning I became slightly concerned when Lakpa casually mentioned that the Everest View Hotel - which I particularly want to see having read so much about it - was not on our itinerary. It would involve only a small detour from the direct route to Namche and so I bring it up during our lunch stop. Several people - a majority in fact - want to visit the hotel. Vivienne didn't appear to be at all interested in my idea. In fact she tried to put us off by saying how long it would take but I think this had the effect of making some of our number even more determined to go. We took a vote which went strongly in favour of a visit. Vivienne gave anyone who didn't wish to go to the hotel the option of taking the direct route back to Namche. But perhaps curiosity or the fear of missing out on something special got the better of the hesitators. The whole group went there together.

There is something entirely repugnant and contemptible about the Everest View Hotel and its background. It was built by a consortium of Japanese businessmen who had spotted a chance to make a quick buck. They could offer people with plenty of money the opportunity to see Everest - as well as Lhotse, Nuptse and Ama Dablam - without having to step outside their hotel. A landing strip was to be built in the immediate vicinity so that customers had no need to trek to the hotel or mingle with local people. This was instant Everest. Or Everest with little or no effort. The appeal was to people who see travel as a way of collecting photographs or videos of themselves standing in front of well-known buildings and places. People with no desire either to explore the countryside or learn about the local population and their way of life.

The construction of the hotel - which opened in 1971 - was a shameful episode. Vast areas of forest had to be cleared and more trees were felled in the locality than had been lost in the whole of the Khumbu region during the previous thirty years. The hotel had to be provided with running water, central heating and electricity for the rich guests. It was the local environment which suffered as a consequence. Call it enterprise if you like. Or call it greed and a mindless disregard for others and for the surroundings.

But sometimes Nature has a way of getting its own back. The businessmen planned a grand opening and invited an Indian television news crew to film it all. Journalists and travel writers from all over the world were invited to stay free of charge. After they had all arrived, the weather took a turn for the worse and no aeroplanes could then land to take them away again. As a result, their stay at the hotel was extended by several days. This did not go down well with busy people who were not used to being away from their desks for long periods.

Much more seriously though, the developers had overlooked the effects of altitude on the human body and especially the effects of flying straight in to a height of fourteen thousand feet. As we all now knew from our own experience on this trek, it is uncomfortable and demanding enough to walk to this height over a number of days involving gradual acclimatization. But to fly straight in is folly. From the airstrip, people had to be loaded onto yaks to reach the hotel. Every room in the hotel had to be supplied with oxygen. Even then, though, there were people who became so unwell that they had to be evacuated. One Japanese woman died. The news spread and understandably the appeal of visiting the Everest View Hotel diminished sharply. On the afternoon we visited it, we had it all to ourselves.

It was a strange experience. We were greeted by friendly, smartly-dressed staff who were kept on to run the place even though there were no guests there at all. We were perhaps their only visitors that day. They seemed pleased to see us, if a little surprised. We inspected the lounge and adjacent rooms. It was all very posh and comfortable compared to the tea houses we had been used to with their bare, basic interiors. At the same time the hotel - for all its opulence - was eerie and cold. Alien too.

We went out onto the balcony for a group photo with Everest in the background. Well, Everest should have been in the background. But the cloud was down.

From the Everest View Hotel our route back to Namche Bazaar takes us through the villages of Khumjung and Khunde. At Khumjung we see the Edmund Hillary School built in 1961 by the Edmund Hillary's Himalayan Trust. At Khunde we visit the hospital also founded by the Trust. More of a health centre in appearance and staffed only sporadically by international volunteers, it provides much-needed basic medical care for the villages in the Khumbu region.

Back in Namche everyone looks relaxed and happy. It has been an interesting and varied day. We've spent most it together whereas on our outward journey we would be splintered and spread out over quite large distances at times. As there is more oxygen in the air and as we are better acclimatized anyway, we've been able to move fast today. Now and again, some of us broke into a run from the sheer joy of just being able to do it.

Namche seems a place of comforts after the bleak and sometimes inhospitable places we've been staying. Here we can sit at tables in a cosy tea house, order a steak and a beer, take the weight off our feet and enjoy the sense of relief that comes with feeling physically better. It's also noticeably warmer down here and we feel assured of a good night's sleep. There's an awareness among us too that our adventure is drawing to a close. Pauline points out that in just five days she will be back at her desk. John and Gwen are expected back at the bank in just four. For the moment though I dismiss any thought of work. I'm determined to enjoy the last few days here in Nepal. I think about how much Jane would have loved meeting the Sherpa people and learning about their lives had she been here with me and I conclude that if I were ever to return here with her I would take things more slowly and acclimatize thoroughly before heading to the higher parts of the region.

Someone reminds us that it's barely three days since our mishap on the Cho La. People are joking about it now as the beer takes hold. Even Mark, who is still wearing plasters on his wounds, smiles with the rest of us. Richard at this juncture does an admirable impression of a sergeant major type with a posh voice reminiscing about his struggles with the dangers of Everest and the challenges of the snow and the ice. It's all very daft of course but funny for all that. In this mood perhaps I'll laugh at anything. One bottle of beer is enough to do the trick after so many days without booze.

# Wednesday 13 October

This morning we all take it easy and pack our things at leisure as Vivienne told us last night that we shan't be leaving Namche until after lunch. We use the extra time to pass around our white hats so that everyone else can sign their names on them. I take more photos of Namche and the surrounding mountains, which are much clearer today than when we were here on our outward journey, for the talks I will give when I get home. I also take photos of anything which might give my audience a clearer idea about our time here, including the yaks, our tents, members of our group and most importantly the people who have guided and supported us. Always at the back of my mind when I take these photos is the thought that one day perhaps this diary will become a book.

Mid-morning one of the climbers, Graham, catches up with us on his way down from Base Camp. He has a badly frostbitten finger which he shows us. It's a gruesome sight actually. He also has a few horror stories about conditions and events high up on Everest. It seems his climbing partner had suffered a great deal on descent and had had to be carried into Base Camp. I wondered at this point whether he ended up in a basket on the back of a porter like Peter had. Worse, it seems that Graham and others had had to bring down a Spanish corpse which was decomposing. I could tell that this had been a traumatic ordeal for him and didn't like to ask why they felt they had needed to bring it down with them, though I would very much like to have known their reasons.

Peter came over to me at one point and asked if I would like to climb the ridge behind the village and have one final look at Everest and the other high mountains. I agreed straight away and off we went, though I did say that I wouldn't want to tarry there too long. He knew why. We now found that we were able to climb to the ridge with surprising ease and talk at the same time. Though the ground was steep we were moving just as easily as we would do back home. What a pity we didn't feel this strong on our way up towards Base Camp, I couldn't help thinking. Once on the ridge we stood side by side and took one last look in silence at Everest with its familiar plume of smoke. We lingered for a few minutes, said goodbye to the world's highest mountain, and then turned to head back to camp.

Word had reached us that Sarah, Duchess of York - commonly known as Fergie - was on her way up to the village with another trekking group. Some of her people had been sent ahead to make preparations for her to be received in due style at one of the tea houses. I'd heard about her trek before travelling out to Nepal. She was to join a group which included a number of disabled climbers attempting one of the lower peaks in the Khumbu region. I didn't know when exactly she was due to arrive at Namche but knowing that she was to fly to Lukla on a particular date, if the weather allowed, I was ready for her. Although I'm no royalist I was determined to meet her. A photo of royalty always goes down well with an audience - and if it doesn't go down well with all of them it does, at least, generate a reaction - and as I was due to give some slide shows on my return home to raise money for Barnardo's I wasn't going to miss out on an opportunity such as this.

We now knew roughly when Fergie was due to arrive in Namche and members of our group duly lined up along the perimeter of our camp - which was on the main path through the village - to observe her from a respectful distance. I however picked up my camera and set off downhill, thinking about what I could say to her if indeed I could get anywhere near her. I had perhaps gone about 200 metres from our camp when I saw her bright red hair glistening in the afternoon sunshine. I hadn't seen any other Westerners for days and she and her group of bodyguards stood out. As I drew nearer and said 'Hello', the four or five stocky males accompanying her - all dressed for hiking - closed ranks around her and eyed me with suspicion, though no-one was actually unpleasant. With a friendly smile, I looked straight at Fergie and confidently uttered something entirely untrue about my mother being a huge fan of the Royal Family and wondered whether she would be so kind as to allow me to take a photograph of her. It must be tiring when people ask you for a photo, I suppose, but she was good enough to oblige.

They all smiled for the pictures and Fergie spoke a few words to me before turning her head away to one of the others. One of her group, inclined to be more friendly than the rest, asked me whether I was trekking in the area. I told him where our group had been and answered some of his questions about conditions higher up. Fergie's attention was elsewhere until I mentioned the name Brian Blessed. This was obviously the password to the royal mind. At this she came alive, took half a step towards me and started questioning me closely about Brian and his whereabouts. It became obvious that she was keen to meet him. I told her as much as I could and enjoyed the feeling of being the focus of her undivided attention for a minute or two and looking her straight in the eye. When she realised there was no more to be gleaned from me about Brian she turned to one of her escorts and suggested they proceed.

Anyway, the photos were in the camera and it was mission accomplished as far as I was concerned. I accompanied their party up the hill as far as our camp, talking to others of her bodyguards who had suddenly found their tongues. The rest of our group were leaning over the low wall of the campsite waving, taking photos and in some cases actually clapping. The few locals who witnessed all this clearly had no idea who Fergie was or what the fuss was all about. My companions probably thought I was a creep. But several of them wanted to know afterwards what she and I had been talking about and were very keen to hear about my encounter with royalty. I had to admit that I'd found her very pleasant and that I'd enjoyed our brief conversation.

In the afternoon we trek gently down from Namche. After an hour or so we reach a tiny place called Chumoa where we spend our last night but one under canvas. In what seems a short space of time we have left the high mountains far behind us. Lukla is now only an easy day's walk away. As we get established in our camp on the side of the main path, we see other groups of Europeans heading upwards towards Namche. The trekking season seems to be getting under way in earnest.

# Thursday 14 October

Today was the final day of our trek, though as it turned out it was not our final day in the foothills of the Himalaya.

The walking now seemed easy to us as we strolled gently downhill towards the spot where we camped at the end of our first day in the region. We soon arrived at the Jenga-like bridge which had looked so rickety and intimidating on our way out. In appearance it was exactly the same now as it was then but no-one seemed in the least bit hesitant about crossing it. All the same, just for the fun of it we sent Gwen ahead of us once again to show us how it should be done.

Soon afterwards we reach the first bridge over the Dudh Khosi river which we crossed on that first afternoon after leaving Lukla. Someone reminds Richard that he has already crossed this bridge three times and he is warned not to make it six times by leaving his rucksack behind again. With a broad grin, Richard straps it very tightly across his chest and sets off ahead of us. No-one looks worried as we approach the bridge today but it still requires care. In fact it appears to me as I cross it that even more of its planks are missing now.

From here it's just an uphill walk of an hour or so to Lukla and it what seems like no time at all we're outside the tea house where we first met Lakpa and the other Sherpas as well as the team of porters. There will be a final get-together for us all tonight. It will be a chance for us to say thank you to them for making our adventure possible. At the same time we'll be saying goodbye.

There's a well-established custom of leaving any unwanted clothing and equipment behind after an expedition as an extra thank you to the Sherpas and porters. So, late afternoon, when we repack our large expedition bags for the last time, all the members of our group place various items in large plastic bags which are then carried over to the main room in the tea house where they will later be given to our support team. I choose several pairs of socks, a hand towel, a pair of grey cords I used to wear for work but which were eventually relegated to the status of walking trousers, some gloves, bin liners and rubber bands. Also among the items I donate is an old pullover given to me by a former girlfriend. It was one of hers actually but she liked to see me wearing it and eventually it became mine. I had decided before coming to Nepal that it was time to part with it once and for all.

The tents have been erected for our final evening here and some people, including me and Peter, head off for an hour's shut-eye before we all congregate in the tea house for our evening meal and for the farewell get-together. Vivienne tells us it's likely to be a long evening.

She wasn't wrong. When we all trouped over to the tea house we found all the support team there in the large, main room. There was something of a party atmosphere. The bags of items we had given them had all been emptied onto the middle of the floor in one huge pile. Tables had been pushed together at one end of the room and our group all sat at these. The Sherpas and porters sat on the benches which lined the walls. It was the first time we had all eaten together, as a matter of fact.

After a splendid meal, we did a presentation of tips to Lakpa and his main team of guides. Then a draw was held among both the Sherpas and the porters for the items we were leaving for them. I wasn't quite sure how this draw worked exactly but everyone was involved and I was quietly pleased that this included the porters as they were not as well paid or as highly regarded as the Sherpas. Each person made a pile of the items that became theirs. Lakpa himself, as a matter of fact, didn't seem to do particularly well and had only a small pile. Some of the porters though did very well. I was tickled when I saw Madhu take that old pullover of mine from the big central pile. She tried it on straight away and obviously felt it suited her. There was a little laughter around me from members of our group who knew where it had come from but Madhu, as far as I know, was unaware of this.

Afterwards the tables and chairs were moved to one side in readiness for the dancing. But first came the singing. The porters began by singing a song in their own language which the Sherpas, I noticed, were not able to join in with. This was followed by a song from the Sherpa women and then a song from all the Sherpas together. They all then signalled to us to sing something. After some initial hesitation, embarrassment and discussion we eventually all attempted a Beatles song. Or was it an old song we had all learned in primary school? My memory is a little hazy, probably due to the beer, the chang and the whiskey which appeared from somewhere. After our song, which we sang very badly, the Sherpas showed us a traditional dance. One of the porters then produced a mouth organ and the merry-making continued until about eleven o' clock when the party eventually broke up.

It was to be a day and a half before we could leave Lukla. The low cloud prevented flights from arriving from Kathmandu. On at least two occasions during the day following our farewell party in the tea house our bags were taken to the landing strip, building up our hopes of a departure. But each time they were brought back. The same happened the following morning. We were all getting to the point where we simply wanted to get away, no matter what the perils of the flight might be. So it was a huge relief to see the cloud break up during the afternoon. We made our way to the landing strip and shortly afterwards our little plane came into view in the distance.

Once the plane had landed and turned around, our bags were stored away for us. By now, although I was desperate to be on my way, I still wanted to have a look around and take it all in for one last time before we set off for the bedlam of Kathmandu. Eventually we were allowed on board and we took our seats. Peter sat next to me as he had done on the outward flight. I noticed we had the same pilot too but this time

Richard passed no comment. As the plane roared its way downhill along the landing strip, passing the wreckage of other planes, I couldn't help thinking of the deep gorge directly ahead of us and wishing she would get the plane up sooner rather than later. Needless to say, it was a perfect take-off. I took one last look back towards the receding snow-covered mountains, looked down into the black chasm as we crossed it and then settled down to the flight back to the capital.

Back in our hotel in Kathmandu the atmosphere is relaxed and celebratory. Amongst the climbers and the members of our group there is also an element of relief. It's always a relief when the whole party returns safely from the mountains and it's good to be sitting in a comfortable chair in a very pleasant hotel holding a bottle of beer and knowing that we will soon be on our way home to Britain.

I'd been hoping to see Brian again. In the event, I heard him before I actually saw him. He came roaring into the hotel bar that evening and before long he was entertaining us all with stories of his climb, how he had refused absolutely to take any bottled oxygen and had, as a result, spent a considerable amount of time on his own at the South Col. He spoke of some of the other climbers and their habits but he spoke most of all about how hard it had been, physically, to get up the Lhotse Face and from there onto the South Col of Everest. As against this he had clearly been impressed by the sheer scale and majesty of all he could see around him.

The next day, after breakfast, we all got on the bus which took us back to the airport. The journey wasn't interrupted by cows. In no time at all, we were on our aeroplane. At one point during the flight home from Kathmandu, when I was sitting next to Brian talking about this and that, I mentioned that I might one day write a book about our trip to Nepal to raise money for charity.

I raised the subject of a foreword for the book and asked if he would consider writing it. 'Anything to help,' was his immediate response.

The train slows down as it approaches the station in Gobowen. As it does so, I look across the tracks to the platform opposite. I see myself sitting alone on the bench very early one September morning nearly a month ago. I see myself fumbling in my pocket for my house key just as I'm doing at this moment. I remember how I was feeling then. I remember - if you like - the person I was then, before the adventure which has added another layer to me. In a few days' time my impressions of daily life in the Himalaya will start to fade, I realise. The familiar routine of normal, everyday life here will replace my recent routine and the proper order of things will be restored. Things will be as they should be once again. In the meantime I can't get out of the habit of looking around every now and then in case there's a yak behind me wanting to pass.

As I get off the train, Jane - reliable as ever - is waiting for me on the platform. There's so much to tell her and I can't help wishing she could have experienced that extra layer with me. I've now seen Everest with my own eyes. It's no longer just something I've read about in books and online and seen in films. In a small and indefinable way it's part of me now. Just like Lakpa, the Sherpas and porters and, yes, Madhu the tea lady.

Jane asks me if I want to drive us home from the station. It feels strange to sit in a car after such a long time and I have to remind myself how to use the controls. Within a minute or less though I've got used to moving my hands and feet again in the correct way. The joy of rediscovery surges through me as I pass familiar landmarks. It's really good to be home.